Spiritual Social Activism

Change the World from Inside and Out with
Spiritual Principles

Sophia Lovgren Ph D

BALBOA.
PRESS
A DIVISION OF HAY HOUSE

Balboa Press books may be ordered through booksellers or by contacting:

Balboa Press
A Division of Hay House
1663 Liberty Drive
Bloomington, IN 47403
www.balboapress.com
1 (877) 407-4847

Because of the dynamic nature of the Internet, any web addresses or links contained in this book may have changed since publication and may no longer be valid. The views expressed in this work are solely those of the author and do not necessarily reflect the views of the publisher, and the publisher hereby disclaims any responsibility for them.

The author of this book does not dispense medical advice or prescribe the use of any technique as a form of treatment for physical, emotional, or medical problems without the advice of a physician, either directly or indirectly. The intent of the author is only to offer information of a general nature to help you in your quest for emotional and spiritual well-being. In the event you use any of the information in this book for yourself, which is your constitutional right, the author and the publisher assume no responsibility for your actions.

Print information available on the last page.

ISBN: 978-1-5043-9719-3 (sc)
ISBN: 978-1-5043-9721-6 (hc)
ISBN: 978-1-5043-9720-9 (e)

Library of Congress Control Number: 2018901489

Balboa Press rev. date: 02/06/2018

Contents

"A highly profound work that will help any student of life find their power, connect with their tribe, chart their course, and rock the world from the inside out."

Mike Dooley,
*NY Times*Bestselling author of *Infinite Possibilities*

In this book I have quite freely used and developed ideas, theories and methods from other people. In many cases there are references, for the reader to read further. In some cases there are not references, since either it is my own ideas or ideas developed further from fellow authors. Not mentioning these authors by name is not equal to not appreciating them. On the contrary, I hold them high. Continuations of the principles, practices and methods introduced in this book can be found on my webistes. Sophia Lovgren

www.sophialovgren.com
www.spiritualsocialactivism.com
www.visionarylife.se

Introduction

To be spiritual is to be political, and to be political is to want something more and better. Not only for yourself but for the whole society. It is the responsibility of a spiritually developed individual to set in motion a movement to fight injustice. Usually it is also at the same time an internal yearning to do so. We are not, with Martin Luther Kings words, "merely a thermometer that record the ideas and principles of a popular opinion, but a thermostat that transform the mores of society". But to question, in order to change, conventional thoughts and behaviours does not come without a cost of loss of for instance status or group belonging. Therefor it is essential for the courageous spiritual social activist to both develop her or his holistic leadership and to find her or his tribe.

This book is focused on evolved and empowered inner wisdom that we both need and yearn to develop, in order to truly and finally create our world from inside and out. By doing so, we may solve both our own challenges in life and problems we are facing in our society of today. We, as spiritual social activists, have a miraculous access to enormous power if we just tap into it. If we use our inner wisdom, that is just waiting for us to act, and also take benefit from existing scientific knowledge in the form of neuroscience and quantum physics, we will transform into powerful spiritual change-makers and evolutionaries. And by doing so, we will once and for all create happiness and abundance for us all – including Mother Earth and nature – which has always been our natural birthright. It is our true nature to live in love, joy and truth.

September 2009 His Holiness the 14th Dalai Lama said, participating in Vancouver Peace Summit, "I am a feminist and I think Western women will save the world". Now the event in itself was a concrete example of the potentiality in female power, since several prominent women participated: peace activist and former Irish president Mary Robinson; founders of the Northern Peace Movement, Mairead Maguire and Betty Williams and anti-landmine crusader Jody Williams. Still, my belief is that Dalai Lama not only referred to the present female participants. Instead I believe that he referred to the fact that it is female energies, that is "typical" female thinking, perspective and approach, that will save the world. And Western women in general undoubtedly have more resources and opportunities to reinforce female thinking, perspective and approach as solutions to save our world, than the rest of the women in this world. But it is a task with great responsibility: our world needs to be truly equal and just.

"We can't solve problems by using the same kind of thinking we used when we created them", as Albert Einstein famously said. And it is perfectly clear that it is masculine energies that has created our existing problems in the world. What problems we now are facing in the world, how female energies might be the problem-solving issue and in what way and how we might proceed will be focus in this book. This is therefore a book for spiritual change-makers and evelutionaries focusing on spiritual social activism. This is a book for you who deeply feels moved to transform into a spiritual social activist, and use your inner wisdom and power as a change-maker and evolutionary.

We have surely all found ourselves in spiritual and sacred situations that has moved us physically, emotionally and spiritually. If not before, then when you hold the small hand of your new-born, and look into the deep, magic eyes of your child, your inner self will be touched in a way that is sacred and spiritual. We can't avoid reflections on our life and on our soul, not even in our high-technical and stressed-out society. We are not only bodies, that needs rest, cleansing and nutrition. And we are not only our capacity to handle numbers or difficult abstract conclusions. We are something more. And this deep feeling of something more, which we cannot see but strongly sense, creates a never-ending longing to show ourselves as the holistic creatures we really are. We long to show ourselves as the perfect souls we are, in truth, joy and love and without shyness, shame or doubt. This is what mankind has yearned for at all times, and tried to show through art, poetry, literature, dance, religion and science.

And as a last introductionary side-note: To be a spiritual social activist does not in any way prevent you from also being a law-obedient citizen. Social activism can in many ways be legal actions to raise awareness of an injustice of any kind, for instance to influence the result of a political decision. At the same time it also has no contraposition with your status or position in your society. You might be a CEO for a large company as well as a high-tech entrepreneur, both examples of positions that might result in large income. There is no contradiction in living within the system, and benefit well from it, which you at the same time critisize and try to change due to existing injustices. I might go so far as to say the larger benefits, the higher responsibility to improve our societal system by both making politicians and decision-makers aware of injustices they might be unaware of and offer support to people in need of help. A spiritual social activism focuses on enhancing every individual's higher potential, by creating a society which supports this instead of opposes it. With spiritual principles in a holistic leadership every individual will be given the opportunity to first lead her or his own life, and the lifes of loved ones, and from there choose to continue to influence, inspire and strengthen other people.

Sophia Lovgren

www.sophialovgren.com
www.spiritualsocialactivism.com
www.visionarylife.se

1. Holistic model of social activism

The new merge of science and spirituality in social activism

We have been taught that we should keep science, spirituality and politics separated, but nothing could be more misleading. Science and spirituality is mainly about the same thing: which is efforts to understand the universe and ourselves. Such efforts will eventually form a thesis on "how things are", from both professors and priests. Unfortunately, it often ends there, with different theories how we should act, think and feel, without any practical solutions of techniques and tactics, which is the task of politic. This explains the situation our world is in today. When we have created our own truth concerning how we comprehend the world, and above all, believes how the world should be, what is more logical then to thereafter try to work politically to make this happen? More often than not, however, the holistic belief does not result in a holistic action.

It is a fact that the world can be so much better than it is today, if we all worked together in bringing all aspects of life together in a holistic approach. Our change of reality is only one thought away. We can almost immediately live in a society that is better, more positive, truer, whilst we ourselves are free in our efforts and mission to live as fully as we can, using our abilities, talents and potential. We just need a critical mass of change-makers and evelutionaries; people who are willing to not only work for themselves to be happy, healthy and wealthy, but who also considers it as important to do their part to create a happier, healthier and more wealthy society, where all inhabitants – human beings and animals – are treated with respect and empathy.

With a holistic model of spiritual social activism we can define different levels that affects us personally – soul, mind and body – but which is also affecting in both our actions and creations in reality as well as society itself. To use this holistic model, is to set up your own agenda how you – with your unique set of talents, capacities and knowledge – shall do your part as a spiritual social activist. You can with this holistic model easily create your own spiritual path as a change-maker or evelutionary in this world, as you also can plan your actions with your tribe.

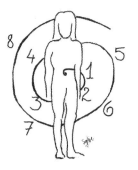

Holistic model of spiritual social activism

1   Emotional Self and Neuroquantology
2   Intellectual Self and Personality
3   Physical Self and Energy
4   Belonging in Love
5   Growth and equal access to dialogue
6   Power and the distribution of resources
7   Safety and the creation of communities
8   Identity and the creation of a holistic world

Holistic model
By Sophia Lovgren

Spiritual principles

Society of today has a lack of moral or ethical guidelines or policies. Western societies has more or less detached from religious leadership and control, even though the majority of all people still have a spiritual belief. To set up your own spiritual principles, is to set up your own spiritual agenda. Nothing, in fact, can be more important than your clarified guidelines for your missions and visions in your life. I will through out the book define spiritual principles, connected to each part or phase in the holistic model, to simplify your own process. Methods to further work with the spiritual principles can also be found in my website. The suggested physical actions that I also present will also continuosly be developed in my website.

The spiritual principles focuses on how you want to define yourself as a spiritual person – in soul, mind and body – in the world of today. The spiritual principles are also completed with practices of freedom, which can be seen as general guidelines for not only yourself, but for your tribe, your family, your neighbourhood, your workplace etc. It focuses not on you as an individual, but on how we should look at and treat each other, regardless of age, gender, ethnicity, religion etc. To simplify the process of making the practices of freedom concrete, I have also suggested some methods of freedom, that is, methods how to for instance make group decisions, how to communicate to each other etc.

Your powers as a spiritual social activist

In this book I describe three different powers for your mission as a spiritual social activist.

I talk about neuroscientific findings, that tells us how imporant it is to focus on the positive aspect of life and how crucial it is to treat our brain as the sharp problem-solver it is – but nothing else. Our brain should be "trained" to mostly solve urgent and actual problems that matter to us and not devote our time with worrying about the future or regretting the past. The more you discipline your brain to focus on constructive, reinforcing ways to live (whether it is a reality yet or not) the more effective tool your brain will be.

Quantum powers is the second power for your spiritual social activism. Quantum physics has for several decades shown us, what we now can express. We are energy beings, living in an energy field, and we can with our focus control and change energy. To use Quantum powers, is to truly accept the possibilities that exist in this energy field. And if we manage to combine our Quantum powers with understanding of neuroscientific conditions, we have a Neuroquantology that will strengthen our Mastershop.

Finally some words about your tribe, the third power, existing or coming into reality. It can of course be a private tribe, with mostly friends, or it can be your professional business or network. It doesn't really matter. Some spiritual social activist will not even know their tribe, that is people who will be inspired by and follow their path. Likewise, your spiritual social activism may or may not be what you get paid for. All spiritual social activists love what they do, are usually great at what they do and the world needs it. This doesn't need to mean you will as well get paid for it. But it certainly means it is your passion and your mission, and you get great satisfaction from doing it.

On my website I am continuosly publishing new findings and research about spiritual social activism, when it comes to new scientific findings in neuroscience and Quantum powers as well as it comes to creating and developing your tribe.

The work I have started with the two roles of change-makers and evelutionaries are also a work in progress. I have in this book presented the most important methods and techniques for evolving in each role.

2. Two types of spiritual social activists

"Darkness cannot drive out darkness; only light can do that.
Hate cannot drive out hate; only love can do that."

Martin Luther King

Spiritual naturals as unstoppable forces

Spiritual naturals are people who have an innate gift or talent for a particular task or activity, and who goes to almost any length to be able to live it out. Spiritual naturals are what we are in fact born to be, but from early age society oppress our inner longing to become what we yearn to become and do what we feel passionate to do. Many of us give up in our strive to realize our own divine possibility on earth. Instead we accept our burden of citizenship, which is to fill our lives with education, work and never ending obligations.

A perfect example of a spiritual natural was Leonardo da Vinci. Da Vinci was an Italian artist, architect, inventor and scientist that was born 1452 in Tuscany and died 1519 in France. He studied different subjects as anatomy, astronomy, mechanic, botanic and geology. You might say he had a creative intelligence that made him curiously thirst for knowledge. His talents were his great fortune and probably also his great sorrow. There is approximately 3,500 pages with drawings, sketches, notes etc., but he seemed to have a problem with completing his works since many of his paintings are incomplete. This may have been due to some kind of anxiety of performing, since most of his works were ordered or about to be sold. One other explanation is that new ideas stole his attention, and made it difficult to finish old ideas. Regardless which, he developed his knowledge in a creative and intuitive flow instead of through rationality and logic. He was obviously very curious, and wanted constantly to understand and explain universe, nature and mankind. Da Vinci was also the type of genius that sometimes behaved irrational, and sometimes even stupid, since he for instance got into arguments with the Catholic Church, partly due to his intense anatomical studies.

Da Vinci was characterised by impulsiveness, risk taking, seeking for sensations, intuition and insights. If da Vinci had lived in our time, it is fully possible that he would have been diagnosed with ADHD as a young child, and even prescribed medicine. People with ADHD shares a genetic similarity with the gene of DRD4 exon III, which encourages risk taking and sensation seeking. The gene plays a key role in the way which the brain regulates dopamine, which affects how we seek adventure and how we use our mental, physical, emotional and spiritual force. Often people with the gene of DRD4 exon III perceives constantly unconscious ideas and impulses, which would require a lot of energy in holding it all back. They also prefer to listen to their inner authority, challenge the norm and break the rules, since they don't accept external authority or conventional hierarchy.

As an opposite group we can see people diagnosed with Asperger's; since they often prefer routines and rules (although preferably their own). In Asperger's, which basis is Autism, there are about 100 genes that seems to influence. Many different genes need to undergo various changes or mutations in their way their DNA is arranged, to create Asperger's. A person with Asperger's usually feel a bit socially awkward and have problems expressing and fully understanding emotions. She or he prefers to have goals and structures, regardless if it is a conversation or an activity, like taking a walk. Often she or he also has one or maybe a few passions of interest, that means more than anything to them. A well-known symbolic character of Autism, that is the basis of Asperger's, is of course Dustin Hoffman in the movie Rain Man, acting as Tom Cruise's older brother.

Rain Man, Raymond, disliked any change in his routines and preferred to only involve himself in his interests and hobbies. This interest however, he was very knowledgeable about. He avoided eye contact and didn't pick up on social cues, as if totally uninterested in the other people that were close to him. But as a contrary, he was overstimulated by loud noises and lights. He himself acted and communicated in a stiff manner, without for instance tone, pitch or accent in his speech, and with a stiff facial expression and posture. Asperger's doesn't obviously has to be seen in body language or in communication styles, but quite often there is a need for the people with Asperger's to intellectually learn how to interact with others. They simply don't have the intuitive and emotional feeling on how to interact, based on picking up emotions and physical reactions in other people. It is not due to any lack of interest in interacting with other people, it is just a lack of central coherence which makes it easy to see small details (colour of eye glasses and shoe laces) but not put all the small details together to grasp a bigger picture.

ADHD and Asperger's are neurodevelopmental disorders, that means it originates from the brain or nervous system and it affects a person's emotions, self-control and social communication and social interaction. That means that it is not possible to actually see the source of either ADHD or Asperger's. You cannot pick up and show the genes as proof. In the same way we don't really know for sure how genes in DNA are structured for every human being, when it comes to specific traits of ADHD or Asperger's. That means that all of us, in fact, might have tendencies of one or the other diagnosis. Maybe we all "in one way or the other" have a faint tendency to either ADHD or Asperger's, instead of the popular belief of a majority of the population defined as "normal"? Often we actually find in both scientific popular literature and coaching advices different labels or categories of mainly two different groups of human beings. There is extroverts or introverts; the A-type group or the B-type group; the hunters or the farmers; the Indigo children or the Crystal children or what other kind of labels there might be.

However, the interesting thing with individuals with what we might define as deficiencies in specific neurotransmitters and/or neurobiological differences or what we might define as spiritual naturals, is that these groups tends to have an unstoppable force in their effort to pursue their internal passions and follow their own and unique process in learning and evolving. These individuals don't seem to have the same strong instinct to belong to the pack and can therefor both recognize and choose to ignore societal norms, principles and structures that is not beneficial or even unjust. This is not meant to be interpreted as a tribute to individuals born with different neurological challenges. Research shows how difficult it can actually be to find one's place in the family and in society, struggling or merely surviving through school and fighting to somehow fit in as an adult. But this is an evidence of a society that needs to change, and a signal for us all to realize that these individuals more than anything teaches us to maintain our birth-right to pursue our possibilities to develop our natural gifts and talents.

We all have a higher potential, connected with our soul, and our purpose in life is more than anything to understand tgis higher potential. And to do this, we need to follow our inner dreams, curiosities and interests in a way that is natural for us. We have all come to this beautiful planet already gifted with incredible strengths, to give joy to ourselves and our family and community. We should devote our lives in finding the best ways to express these talents. I will introduce my suggestions for developing our higher potential, in the form of two different "spiritual roles": Change-makers and Evelutionaries.

"Wired the way we are" for a reason: neuroscientific spirituality

Our brain consists of approximately 100 billions nerve cells that are called neurones. Each neurone has between 1 000 and 10 000 synapses, that is, places that connects with other neurones and creates network. We can call these networks a neurone net, and a simple description would be that it represents a thought, a memory, an ability etc. All neurone nets are connected to each other in different ways, and these connections builds up complex ideas, memories and feelings. When stimuli comes in from our surroundings the neurone nets starts to work, which will start a chemical change in the brain, which will create an emotional reaction. When we again and again repeat certain behaviour, that specific neurone net will develop a stronger connection, which will make it easier to connect that neurone net. In this way good and bad habits will come automatically. In the same way "the furrow will not get ploughed", if we stop certain behaviour, since that specific neurone net will cease "its relation". A brain with only a few furrows will result in a unchangeable and extreme personality, but fortunately our brain has neuroplasticity; a natural ability to bend up connected neurone nets and break old habits. It is very important with neuron plasticity, since a flexible brain will create geniality, creativity and intuition.

Neuroscience is the science about our brain and how it decides moment by moment what is most relevant to notice, observe and focus. The brain's primal drive forces is to minimize threats and maximize rewards. This affects us in our attitudes and behaviors to situations and people. If we perceive threats, we will choose fight, flight or freeze. If we perceive rewards, we will show interest and curiosity. By understanding this process, we can choose to reward our brain. This we do by becoming aware about our thoughts and emotions. Our emotions are the navigation system for our brain, and activates without us being aware about it. The emotions sends signals to our brain, which distributes hormones and signal substances to our body, which in turn mobilizes to behave in specific ways. It is a feedback system between the external world and our individual brain and body. When we identify this process, we receive thoughts and thereby we can choose how to act and respond. This however requires our conscious mind and will.

Our brain is constantly seeking our social and physical surrounding, to find signals that can imply positive or negative consequences for us. This in turn creates an emotional charge, that affects all processes that our brain is involved in. The problem is that our brain have five times higher probability to negativity, which is inherited since our survival depends on our ability to quickly perceive possible threats. In other words, we human beings focus five times more often on negative information or experiences, than on positive information or experiences. This knowledge gives in itself emphasis on the importance of acting in love. When we act with tenderness and respect towards other human beings, we create an atmosphere of trust and meaningfulness. This "calms down" our brain, since it needs not look for danger, and by doing this we can actually build up a more sharpened focus. With loving actions we will become more intelligent. I will in the following chapters in more detail present the holistic model av spiritual social activism, which in different ways actualizes loving actions with optimal conditions for our brain to be the sharp tool it is meant to be.

The much needed balance between Yin and Yang energies

Our society of today consists of processes that reinforce or thrive on masculine energies, due to a supressed spirituality, our stressful and anxious time of post-modern capitalism and a never before seen increased consumption of products and experiences. These societal forces affect and reshapes us individuals in a way that encourages our aggressive, straight-forward and somewhat ruthless traits. Our suppression of the feminine energies has gotten so severe that we are now on the edge of destroying Mother Earth herself, and of course consequently ourselves.

So what does masculine and feminine energies mean more specific? Masculine energies can in many ways be described as yang, which is an intellectual and analytical energy that primarily uses thoughts. Yang starts from a linear and historical time, and prefers numbers and obvious connections between reason and effect. Yang creates energy and activity, but also brutality and ruthlessness. A feminine energy can be described as Yin, which is a way of thinking that comes from experiences and shows itself in different shapes, which is an untouchable and magical form with a circular (non-linear), timeless and eternal time. Yin creates receptiveness, understanding and warmth, but it might also create submission, mobbing and obsession. Both women and men can be dominated by either Yang or Yin. A spiritual master lets both energies exist, and use them consciously depending on what is more suitable in each situation. Neither energy is better than the other, but has its natural place in any given situation. You are simply in one way as a human being when you care for your baby, hug your grandmother or talk with your best friend, than you are when you are holding an important lecture in front of a large audience, brainstorming with your colleagues before a meeting with a big client or studying before an examination.

We consist of body, intellect and soul. We have access to both masculine and feminine energies. We are a holistic "she-he". That doesn't mean that we all have similar access to masculine and feminine energies. Depending on our biological body, our self (personality, talents, strengths) and our spiritual maturity, we will have a tendency to more often use one of the two energies. This unique combination is continuous altering, depending on how we are facing specific situations. In a tolerant context we will aim to reach a more balanced, harmonic and holistic life. The body alone will never be the sole source influencing what kind of energy we will prefer; just because you have a male body it doesn't mean that you will prefer masculine energy.

Yin energies in action can feel very threatening to a person that only relies on scientific, technological knowledge. To be rational towards life means to calculate life, to use one's logical sense in life. It is nothing wrong with this, if it wasn't for the fact that we almost only praise and depend upon our rational, logical self. We have with our focus on rationality almost destroyed this planet, and we have spent a lot of years killing and intimidating each other. We should not use our logical reasoning in life; we should live our life with a certain logical reason. But above all we should live with our inner truth and inner leadership. We need to find our intuition, and empower this intuition, and with our inner leadership create a balance, and fill our world and Mother Earth with empathy, respect, acceptance, love, light and creativity.

We may characterize Yang energy as not only a kind of masculine energy, but with a "hardware" functionality, where you will find measurability, comparability, performance, competition and hierarchy. This energy find numbers important and it is with this energy you create the demand to be effective or the need to strive for a career. More often than not this energy reinforces initiative from experts or initiated people, often with demands on both economical and resourceful development, which is preferably built on some kind of expertise knowledge.

We may likewise characterize Yin energy as not only a kind of feminine energy, but with a "software" functionality, where you will find feelings, relations, balance, satisfaction and intimacy. This energy find experience important and it is with this energy you create the longing after a meaning or the need to rely on your own gut feeling. More often than not this energy reinforces initiative from the people, often with no demands on profit nor development, that is built on organic process of knowledge.

Yin and Yang energy explained with four different ways of behaviours

Yin energy can be divided into two main categories:

- **Visuals** are extremely passionate and inspire other people to care about issues they themselves care about, but in moments of stress or conflicts they focus on facts which can undermine their ability to empathize with the other person.
- **Digitals** are rational and principled people and they have a gift for quickly understanding complex situations. In moments of stress or conflicts they can become closed to other peoples perspectives and feelings.

Yang energy can also be divided into two main categories:

- **Kinesthetics** are generous, compassionate and accepting of other people but their caring nature can pull them into too many directions. Therefore they may meet other peoples need at the expense of their own needs, which eventually cause mounting resentment.
- **Tonals** have a gift for understanding other people and their dilemma, but their ability to read between the lines can morph into hearing what was never said, felt or thought.

Spiritual Change-makers and Evelutionaries

Yin and Yang energy can also be described as natural energies creating your behaviou, in terms of spiritual social activism. With intentions of spiritual social activism I have developed from yin and yang energies two different kind of spiritual social activists, both equally important but fundamentally different in their life purpose and missions. I will here shortly introduce the two types, to continue defining them in the last chapters of this book. You may also read further information on my research about these types on my website.

Spiritual change-makers are reactively acting, that is they are trying to change an injustice or a problem by building on opinions of solidarity, loyalty, justice and democracy. Change-makers have a yang energy, which can produce a tendency to risk-taking and sensation-seeking. Their drive force is to listen to their inner voice, even though it might demand breaking rules. The dominant traits are competitiveness, activeness, boldness and straightforwardness. This is the typical extrovert person, meaning outgoing, sociable, people-oriented and unreserved.

Spiritual evelutionaries has a natural talent are creatively creating, that is they are focusing on the flow of life. Evelutionaries have a yin energy, with warmth and receptiveness, and deeply seeks many ways to interact with other people. The dominant traits are nurturing, consideration, empathy, passiveness, non-violence and kindness. This is the typical introvert person, meaning reserved, self-reflexive, inward-oriented and observational.

Regardless of which energy a spiritual natural might be, it is the passion to understand and create the meaning of life that drives her or him. It is a search for her or his inner truth that evokes the strongest feelings and which also in itself creates courage and self-respect. This process strengthen her or his ability to power, passion and creativity.

Spiritual change-makers and spiritual evelutionaries

Illustration with inspiration from medieval drawing of female Sejd (clairvoyant women)

By Sophia Lovgren

The Spiritual Change-makers wants to seek new ways to do ways and needs to find new pathways and solutions. There is a strong adventurous side to the change-maker, who also enjoys hectic environments and big crowds.

The Spiritual Evelutionaries have no desire to seek new outposts in the world, but instead prefer to search inwards. This to both find better understanding of themselves and find better ways to help and support other people. Problem-solving and inner monologues are usually what makes them engaged and motivated.

3. IDENTITY and the creation of a holistic world

"Capitalism does not permit an even flow of economic resources. With this system, a small privileged few are rich beyond conscience, and almost all others are doomed to be poor at some level. That's the way the system works. And since we know that the system will not change the rules, we are going to have to change the system."

Martin Luther King

Identity concerns "the big context". This has to do with citizenship, city and country and with different areas like governance and law, science and technology, environment and infrastructure or social justice and security. Identity issues also focuses on energy, food and water, which is crucial for us. Identity can at the same time concern professional status when it comes to different trades. All these issues affect us profoundly and since it often can be great differences between for instance more economically developed countries, like Western countries, and least developed countries, it also has far spread consequences on us as citizens. Ultimately it is a question about feeling worthy or not, depending on "who you are".

Most of the problems we face in our society depends on a holistic approach in order to be solved. We need therefor to use scientific and technological knowledge as well as psychological and spiritual wisdom. Unfortunately, we have in our pursuit of the first, completely ignored the second. Human kind has in historic times almost solely relied on nature, gods and biological conditions which over time has been replaced by zealous reliance in science and the seemingly wonderful miracles of our technical knowledge and expertise. Spiritual wisdom and scientific knowledge have been effectively separated. Our modern world of today consist of different spheres and forums, without any visible bridges between them. We strive for a formal education and successful career, but it rarely has anything to do with our beliefs in a God or our own struggles with personal challenges. Our intellect may be highly praised, but there are seldom praises for a well-connected self. We may also work intensely with ourselves, being disciplined with mindfulness and meditations, and have a highly developed talent as coach or advisors, but more often than not this is clearly separated with efforts to also change our society or with political ambitions. Likewise, there are many politicians of today that act selfishly, rude, immature… and may even be proud of winning some votes in acting this way, without any demands to act responsibly towards humanity, nature or future societies. The problem is that our outer world has long time ago been separated from our inner world. Now is the time for bringing it all together.

From active citizens to depressed consumers

In our postmodern society we seem to be more "valuable" as individuals than citizens. Our identity and our local context has become more of a matter of choice than of heritage. We have the freedom – and the curse – to decide where and how we want to live, where and how we want to work etc. Obviously this is mostly common for citizens of Western society, but there is a common demand on people to try to create better lives for themselves instead of "just surviving" as it were in the old times. There is also a new understanding of the world. There is a global concept of other societies, not existing before. We might say that globalization has definitely reached its peak, with internet accessible even for poor people in underdeveloped countries.

In Western society this great life of choices in our modern capitalistic world can give individuals unique and exciting possibilities, but it can also create great anxiety for the people who feel they have chosen the wrong alternatives or don't have what it takes to choose and be successful. Therefore, it should not come as a surprise that depression, suicidal dilemma and problems of abuse is common health problems in our society. Suicidal attempts by our young people has skyrocketed the last decade. At the same time, we have other severe health problems connected to our modern way of living, when it comes to what we consume or how we use our body. This "physical degeneration" together with our loss of local context, stability and security creates individuals with almost no connection to family, upbringing, traditions and other locally fixated routines and guidelines but with a never-ending connection to networks, forums, groups, trends – however almost all of them are mostly unstable, short-term and impersonal. We have undergone a transformation from active citizens with self-evident right to influence and protest, to passive consumers; burdened and depressed by the fact that our inherent yearning to create and impact are suppressed and unwelcome.

From power through possessions to power through expertise

Today it is possible to imagine media or social media ridiculing someone for being stupid or intolerant (that is, not having the right knowledge), although he or she is a millionaire. That would have been impossible just ten years ago, let alone 50-100 years ago. It is not any longer only a question of what you have, but also a question of who and what you know. Dominance and societal power is about existing or being absent from important networks, and the person with real power is the one that "operate" the united points of different networks. An example of this are our young youtubers; followed and admired by millions of people. Virtual networks is a new phenomenon in a capitalistic, globalized economy, which has developed an endless deconstructed and reconstructed culture as well as conquered space and exterminated time. Karl Marx, a famous philosopher from early 19th century, skilfully described the capitalists and workers of that time, which in quickly growing cities tried to be richer alternatively survive. This phenomenon still exists, but in the form of global capital network. This global capital network still shapes capitalist's behaviour through constant processes of information. This relates to the network of political actors and the political sphere as well as to the system of mass media; where money, politic and communication seems to dance an intense dance of power. Complex networks contains information that can be exchanged and which connect individuals, institutions and movements. What is illustrated as crucially important, is the ability to find, get access to and understand the right information. This factor has created a vast gap between those who are inside and those who are outside.

The modern cooperate world of today can be described as a system with demands of constant general profit and free exchange of money. The process from caring for and supporting each individual's well-being and constructive integration to a productive and adaptable citizen, to caring for and supporting each cooperate business for the sole purpose of profit has been extreme and brutal. Historically we can see many examples of extreme processes, for instance during colonization, during industrialism and in later time during failures with the stock market, the crisis of the banks and the development of Internet. What is new is the dualism that has become more evident for each decade. The longing after a meaning in life has been replaced with a demand to be successful and effective. Competition and measurability is seen as more important than intimacy and experience. And this is in large due to the patriarchal society that is built on hierarchy, inequality and dualism. If we connect the dominance of the masculine energy to the economical foundation, we will find inhumane examples like war, genocide and persecution of indigenous groups for the same reason: to dominate, rule and conquer. For a long period of time expressions of consciousness, intention, feeling, sense and soul has been living evidence of a weak, unproductive and worthless population. Women in general or indigenous groups has been perfect examples of citizens that has not been seen as important contributors to society in a preferred way; that is, as soldiers, factory workers, minors, sailors or other groups that were both willing and capable of sacrifice themselves for the interest of one's country.

Economic progress versus planet Earth

Along with this destructive progress of our social and economic development we can also see the same hostile tendency to Mother Earth itself. Problems with the global climate is on its way to cause casualties in species in a degree that is comparable with the catastrophe that for 65 million years ago exterminated the dinosaurs. Western people's "ecological footstep" is so demanding for the environment, that we actually need more planets like Earth to survive in the long run. Species is exterminated in a speed that is many times higher than that which would have been, had it been "normal environmental conditions". This depends partly on the intrusion of mankind in places where these species once were thriving, and partly on the changes of the climate. The North pole and practically all the world's mountain glacier are on the verge of melting down. This can cause serious shortage of water for the people living around these glaciers. The large inland ices on Greenland and Antarctic is becoming instable. The streams in the ocean and in the air, which have been stable for almost 10,000 years, is because of this changing.

The relation between the earth and sun is about to change, since we are letting out so much carbon dioxide that the temperature in the earth's atmosphere has increased. This is being absorbed by the oceans and therefore also disturbing all sea creatures' skeleton and shell. We are experiencing a radical increase of algae and other life forms (for instance mosquitoes) carrying different diseases. It isn't difficult imagining how intolerable our lives would be, with great areas of land for ever gone under water, together with constantly threatening weather conditions and threats from animals with different kind of diseases. The global warming has created both flooding and droughts (the precipitation hasn't only increased, but also relocated), and at the same time the great ice shelf of Arctic is about to melt. The great ice shelf of Antarctic as well as the permafrost is also at risk of melting. For the first time ever polar bears has drowned, since there are too few ice shelves. The amount of cyclones has increased dramatically. The durability and length of the large storms has increased by 50 percentages during the last thirty years in both the Atlantic Ocean and the Pacific Ocean. This has resulted in a change of the natural rhythm in the earth's changes of the seasons.

So why are we not acting faster when it comes to facing these challenges? The problem isn't that the scientists are disagreeing about the causes to the changes of the climate. The problem is that multinational companies through mass media constantly are trying to rewrite fact into possible theories. As the famous quote goes (Upton Sinclair): "It is difficult to get a man to understand something, when his income is depending on that he won't understand it". It should not only be environmental "warriors", independent politicians and brave scientists that are warning about a close catastrophe. We all must choose consciously, before earth is facing its destruction. Mother Earth is not an endless resource, and we must stop thinking with such a short-sighted perspective. We need leaders with an inner authority; a loving economy that prioritizes life and its complexity, and an unselfish businessman ship. Our economy as we know it need to be radically changed, since we need a new system that builds on spiritual principles, which include all living things and is based on the cycle in nature and of life. Mother Earth is something we only have as a loan, and therefore we need to create a healthy relationship to nature and to the animals. We need to be in, and feel and listen to, nature, since it develops higher levels of consciousness. Multinational companies don't care about the regrowth of Mother Earth, and we can therefore not turn to them for healthy solutions. What we need to do is to listen to and act upon our own inner leadership and the truth of the soul.

Identity and principles for Spiritual Social Activism

Suggestions for mental and emotional actions, in terms of reflecting for yourself and discussing with your tribe following spiritual principles:

o   **Responsibility**, to do what is right.
o   **Trust**, and rest on knowing what is right.

o **Accountability**, to take responsibility for our activities and results.

o **Freedom**, where we constantly demonstrate the right to act, speak and think.

o **Honour**, in showing integrity to individuals' beliefs and actions.

o **Commitment**, in our dedication to our causes and activities.

o **Observation**, to take note of facts in order to study and learn.

o **Truth**, to that which is unchangeable, consistent and indisputable.

o **Obedience**, with existing laws and authorities.

Try to clarify the most important spiritual principles and in what way you will honour them.

Suggestions for physical actions for yourself and your tribe:

Change-makers	Evelutionaries
Plant green plants in the nearest park and gather your tribe to nurture them	Gather your tribe and offer free meditation in a mall
Meet local politicians and discuss components like happiness and joy as ruling strategies for new political agenda	Collect small gifts (stones with loving messages etc.) and give to your neighbors
Offer to set up bee hives on roof tops and manage them during the year	Take people out, who aren't mobile by themselves, for a trip to the park or to the forest

4. SAFETY and the creation of communities & tribes

"We must become bigger than we have been: more courageous, greater in spirit, larger in outlook. We must become members of a new race, overcoming petty prejudice, owing our ultimate allegiance not to nations but to our fellow man within the human community."

Haile Selassie

Safety focus "the small context", it concerns for instance your workplace, your community, neighborhoods, residential areas, schools and preschools. It also has to do with your local supermarket, your closest park and different kinds of public domains. It is in our local context, with its familiar milieu, sounds and smellings, that we build up our feeling of safety, obviously not regarding the primary trust evolving from family, upbringing and home situation.

Abstract trust and local distrust

Individuals in Western society has with internet and virtual reality created new distances and new type of relations to other people, networks, organisations, companies and authorities. Globalisation is a phenomenon that in its movement has both intensified international relations and transformed local structures. We have become *glocal* citizens, which famous sociologists like Anthony Giddens and Zygmunt Bauman has stated. This is all happening through our new policy to time and space. In our old society, both social relations and personal life was closely connected to time and space; "the when-marker" was connected to "where" and "what" (for instance Sundays meant church-visits in the village and reaching adulthood meant marriage and family). Even small routines were adjusted according to this structure; you paid your bills daytime in the bank; you called your friends when you were free from work and at home. Now we use Internet banks, mobiles and mail where and when we want, we don't have to have routines that is ruled by daylight or season. *Time* and *space* are still important components, but we don't seem to need *place* anymore in our modern society. We can today move where we want to, but still keep our old social relations alive (within certain limits and during some conditions).

The "emptying" of time and space is not the only phenomenon that characterises us modern people. Our before stable and concrete social system has also lost its context. One example of this is our economical transfers, where we besides coin and bill also now uses credit and bitcoin, that is not depending of time or space. In the same way we have diminished social systems, that before was the central point in our social map. We knew and trusted our doctor, our priest and our teacher, and knew we could always turn to them when we needed advice and support. Now we trust "abstract experts" in a way that would be impossible for rural people: We write to, read and trust advices from experts in different magazines. We hear newscasters talk about the latest research on food, health and human bodies, which we with an absent-minded way listen to and then repeat to our friends and colleagues. We walk into the elevator in our house, and quickly see the sticker on the wall that says that the elevator is meant to be inspected within a month, and we count on this to happen, so that the elevator will be safe to use also next year. We pay our bills through Internet bank, and we don't ponder if the transactions will happen or not. We show with other words an enormous trust in abstract relations and structures.

At the same time, we have with our increasing glocal trust strangely enough started to have more doubts; which sometimes have replaced our ability to rationalise. With this new freedom, we have created reflexivity in our lives. We have been given an opportunity to, but also been forced to, reflect over our choices. We have, from our experience, learnt that we cannot trust other people, which means that when something seems to be "too good", we quickly assume that it can't be true. Therefore we never really know for sure what the "right" way is, and this realisation fills us with anxiety and doubt. Since we cannot trust our traditions and habits, we have in this mysterious complexity of choices and possibilities developed a "reflexive I". This reflexivity helps us individuals to choose our "belongings" all the time, to create the ultimate life and avoid the risks that exist in an uncertain and constantly changing society. That is, those of us who can choose, and those of us who makes the "right" choice. With other words, those of us who has money and/or the right contacts. You may participate in the world's most glorious ride, and enjoy it, as long as you can pay for it.

Intersectionality and cooperating techniques of domination

I have described our unjust society, but there are many different categories of discrimination. Intersectionality, coined by Kimberlé Williams Crenshaw, is a term that describes how different systems of domination relates to each other. Multiple identities intersect and creates a whole, which includes different categories as men-women, white-colored, heterosexual-homosexual, rich-poor, young-old etc. In other words, an African-American homosexual woman in her 50'ies will face many different kinds of oppression and discrimination. In this way we can understand injustice and social inequality from a multidimensional perspective. All different kinds of oppression work together and creates a complex system.

This means that it is difficult to work against the whole system of oppression. Often law and policies only manage to address one of the marginalized identities. Gender, age, class, race etc. is categories that often includes one positive, superior label and one negative, inferior label. All these personal categories are of course also addressing groups and larger contexts. If mostly women (defined with an inferior label) works in a specific job, with almost no men (defined with a superior label), the job itself will be stigmatized as inferior. This is a matter of anything in our society (countries, cities, residential areas, clothes, fashion, TV shows, magazines etc.) that in any way can be defined as belonging to either one superior or one inferior category. Even languages, knowledge and belief system are either connected to a superior or inferior group.

The deadly signs of groupthink

Why have so few politicians and decisions-makers shown signs of inner leadership and acted upon the alarming signs of reality? This is due to the phenomenon of groupthink, initially researched by Irving Janis. Groupthink is when a group makes a wrong decision due to group pressure, that in itself lead to decade the group's mental effectiveness, perception of reality and moral judgements. Groups that are characterised by groupthink ignore alternatives and takes irrational decisions. The group ignore warnings and don't consider other alternative solutions. Groupthink happens especially easy when the members of the group are homogenous, when it comes to gender, age, culture, religion, class etc. In other words it is high risk of groupthink when a group consists of almost only white heterosexual men over the age of 50, from middle or upper class Christian upbringing. This however describes most Western societies' Congresses and Parliaments, as well as the EU and FN. These groups is at high risk to create stereotype enemies, that needs to be conquered. This can for example be feministic groups, LBTQ movement or environmental networks. Internal power forbids expressed doubt and hesitation, which leads to a belief that the group's opinion is the opinion of the majority in society.

Examples of group think is the USA:s inability to foresee the attack on Pearl Harbour, the development of the war in Vietnam and the efforts to save the hostage in Iran. More recent examples is Bush's decision to invade Iraq, where it for instance had been more reasonable to seek cooperation amongst the allied. These limited decisions has cost many lives, a lot of money and decreased trust from the rest of the Western society. When it comes to the last example, it is also easy to see that other areas in the society than the political are affected by groupthink, for instance mass media and science. This you can see in badly conducted investigating journalism alternative research, by journalists or researcher that has already chosen sides and thus excluded other alternative. To prevent groupthink you must choose a leader who has his or her genuine contact to inner leadership and choose group participants with great heterogeneity when it comes to gender, age, culture, religion, class. Groupthink is a dangerous phenomenon in the society of today, since it is actually slowly killing us.

Tribes and intention of the group

To prevent intersectionality and group think, we need to both find our own and support other peoples tribes. With our tribes, whose members of course doesn't need to live close, we will be able to create end strengthen the feeling of safety through a glocal context. If you don't have nor belong to a tribe, it will surely come to you. It can already exists within your family or your friends (your framily), but otherwise it is people you will meet and almost immediately feel a special connection to. Probably you will know by heart what special bonds are connecting you, and thereby also your mutual mission.

We are the community

Photo
By Sophia Lovgren

Safety and principles for Spiritual Social Activism

Suggestions for mental and emotional actions, in terms of reflecting for yourself and discussing with your tribe following spiritual principles:

o **Courage**, in doing what is required or necessary to show willingness and ability to do what seems frightening.
o **Ownership**, in our responsibility and accountability for what we think, feel and behave.
o **Alignment**, to create congruency and harmoniously integration with our thoughts, words and actions.

27

o **Optimism**, when it comes to hopefulness that good things will unfold to our mutual benefit.

o **Awareness**, to create knowledge and recognition of a certain situation or fact.

o **Belief**, in that we together can change the world, by create habitual thought patterns about what we hold to be true.

o **Humility**, in remembering our place in context of the whole.

o **Determination**, in supporting the desired process to create desired choices and behaviours.

o **Perseverance**, in our thought and behaviour despite difficulties and obstacles.

o **Simplicity**, recognizing basic needs and requirements.

Try to clarify the most important spiritual principles and in what way you will honour them.

Suggestions for physical actions for yourself and your tribe:

Change-makers	Evelutionaries
Make some lemonade and offer for a hug all who passes by.	Give anonymously flowers or compliments to your co-workers.
Gather your tribe and perform spontaneous loving events.	Offer free meditation or yoga to co-workers before meetings.
Offer free lectures to schools, in the subject you know best.	Collect food people or shops are willing to give away, cook something delicious and give for free.

5. POWER and the distribution of resources

"To deny people their human rights is to challenge their very humanity.
As long as poverty, injustice and gross inequality persist in our world, none of us can truly rest."

Nelson Mandela

Power and the distribution of resources deals with basic fundamentals as learning and education but also the continuation of those fundamentals which leads into work, business and economics. It is here we as individuals can strive for money and possessions, and even make investments, but it is also here we gain and develop our knowledge and status. Power is the force that helps you transform and evolve, and steer your life in the direction where you want to go. Power is both social and political, since it is the ability to influence people or events.

We are all human beings. We are all born with human rights, that is focused on our physical, social and emotional survival and well-being. We are according to human rights born free and equal, and therefore we have the right to a nationality and to think and believe what we want and also express these thoughts and beliefs. We also have the right to physical survival, with food, shelter, rest and sleep, as well as the right to education, to privacy and to play and socially interact.

Our society of today however is characterised by a destructive injustice, which is based on a very simple dualism: they who have and they who don't have; they who are worth getting and they who are not worth getting. Now there are many dualistic examples: man-woman, white-coloured, heterosexual-homosexual, Western society-Eastern society, rich-poor, strong-weak, young-old, adult-child, culture-nature, logic-intuition, intellect-soul. Regardless which opposite you focus on, it stands clear that none of us really gains anything on this unbalance. On the contrary, none of us can live a whole life as long as this unbalanced and unjust structure exists.

One aspect of domination and subordination

As an example we will look at the dualism of gender. Most of us are born with either male or female genitals. Gender is usually the first thing observed on a new-born. And when we know the gender, we have consciously or subconsciously chosen one of two approaches toward the new baby. We are socialised into our role of gender, which gives us a certain behavioural pattern when it comes to for instance appearance and personality. It is difficult to objectively see this behaviour pattern since it is self-evident for us, but if you oppose towards this behaviour it can create strong feelings. We don't learn this behavioural pattern in our childhood alone (how we act in day-care, school and at home). The rest of our lives we will (re)create these roles in our daily interaction with other people (in our family, at workplaces and in the public room). If we cross the limits, we will meet protests or we will be redefined in a way that usually are not satisfying for us.

We can find this self-evident perspective on male and female behaviour in schools, in families and on workplaces. Girls nicely put up their hand, and boys scream right out, when they want to answer the teacher's questions. Women take the majority of sick-leave when their children are sick, which usually affect their career in a negative way. Women are still too few in numbers in all leadership positions. Men have the power to define crucial conditions in the social, economic and private sphere. Several areas is still characterised by giving men precedence. The majority of all leaders, regardless of sector and education, are men. This has affects on personal income, where women consequently earn less money. This of course is worsened for the large group of women who choose or find themselves forced to work part-time, due to main (and sometimes sole) responsibility for family and household. Women are usually also discriminated with a lower income and worse security rights with part-time employments and more limited possibilities to start their own company, since both banks and other loan givers as well as themselves doubts their capacity for success. This unbalance when it comes to leadership roles increases the negative effects for both gender, but also for companies and our society. It is not healthy nor long-term successful for a company to rely on a dominance of one perspective; on one way of thinking. Also, it increases the risk for group-think.

First and second degree citizenships

Women usually have double jobs, since they often have the main responsibility for the children, when it comes to sickness, meetings with school, homework etc., but also when it comes to household chores like laundry, food, cleaning etc. The women's pulse generally goes up when they quit their job, because then it is time to pick up their kids, buy groceries and cook food. Besides these necessary and often stressful activities, they usually also take care of their older and sick relatives. Men's pulse inspelad often gets slower when they finish their job, because then it is time to eat and watch TV. They know they can take it easier, after a hard day of work. Women's double job creates an exposed situation since they tend to have a constant "bodily readiness", where they are always ready for never ending demands for comfort, pleasure and service. They often have a constant "required attentiveness", since they are the responsible adult (in a household with two adults) who listens to and care for family members. Women are usually the ones remembering the children's homework, the date of a friend's wedding and at which relative next Christmas was decided to be celebrated. There is never an end to all obligations, which in the end may results in for instance chronic stress, chronically pain in the muscles etc.

Women still take the majority of the responsibility of the children. This may be seen as desirable for many reasons in the nuclear family, but in single-parent-families it can create severe negative effects. The father is at higher risk to take little or no responsibility for their own children after separation or divorce. Economically this of course may increase the mother's poverty, or risk of poverty. Emotionally, this decreases the children's well-being during childhood, since the psychical loss of one parent affects the child's own self-image and self-love. The mother is also at risk in remaining in poverty or low economic situation, since her double responsibility has negative consequence on her chance for a career. And the father is of course at risk at a negative self-image, even though he might not realize it in the beginning, as a parent with poor contact with his children.

The structure of gender, which is the discrimination by sex according to a patriarchal pattern in society, has become more invisible and thereby harder to question or confront. There is of course not a "secret society of patriarchal men", but there is culturally normative values and standards, informal creations of groups, alliances, loyalty etc. These phenomena can only be distinguished with the help of its consequences (like who is making a career in the company; who is hired; who gets a higher income), but since every consequence can have both a gender characterised and a gender neutral explanation there is an invisibility created that both individualize and privatize. There is a socially invisible pattern, with silent rules, which weakens the visibility in research, mass media and politics. It is the group men that is the standard, and the group women that is the exception; where the men have the authority to define reality and to control the power in the social, economic and private sphere. It is according to the dominant groups' conditions that we discuss gender, power and structure, which thus increases the risk for discrimination to be further invisible.

Women still don't have "full" citizenship. Women are seen as second degree citizen, and "female dimensions" like unpaid work as mothers and caregivers are still not defined as a vital part of a citizenship. Of course men also lose due to this unbalance. Most men obviously have mothers... and usually also a wife, a girlfriend, a sister, a daughter or a female friend. All families, where there is at least one person who is female, should see themselves as discriminated by the patriarchal system. The only logical way is a society where women have economic, social and political equality together with men.

Techniques to conquer and rule

Power is not any longer equal with a certain institution (kingdom) or to certain ability (king), but exists through media and social media in all social and societal relations. This exerted power contains both an intention from the practitioner (that is, a reason for wanting power) and an attitude (within the practitioner; may it be an institution, a department, politicians etc.) to that which is supposed to be controlled. We may call this form of societal power and governing *governmentality*; that is a mentality about governance. This disciplinary power is not only suppressive since it has close relation to knowledge and "truth": In order for a state to rule its population, it needs detailed knowledge about them, and thereafter it needs well functioned machines that will implement "truths" about human behaviour, that the citizens accepts. This specific kind of governance can occur through freedom, that is we individuals can be encouraged (by political authorities or different kind of experts) to take our own initiative, but "persuaded" (with a hint of reprisals) to make the *right* choices. What is created is controlled consumers that "must" live what is defined as good lives, and where possible setbacks are defined as our own fault.

Both political and non-political forces rule with the help of standards and sanctions (besides law and constitution) through individual's needs, interests and opinions. It is not only a question about the government, but instead a complexity of techniques and strategies from an invisible hierarchy of power. Our actions are formed, by ourselves and others, through our way of thinking, feeling and perceive ourselves. We are drowned by the abundance of possibilities, the most when it comes to consumption, but at the same time we shall also protect ourselves from all the suggestive and unconscious commercial and be able to take the right decisions when it comes to work, career, food, sport, leisure time, culture, economy etc. Whatever we might do that is wrong, we are unable to blame the government or the free market, even though they both makes a profit due to our feeling of being lost.

Our society of today is in high degree built on differences, which historically was class, gender and ethnicity. Today it is also about knowledge and status in different networks. Our societal structure is built and formed on the acknowledgement of differences, rather than on similarities. This acknowledgement of difference can focus on different subjects; like segregation and different types of suburbs, poverty and reasons for unemployment or violence and tendencies to be a certain type of victim. The accepted belief is that there is one group who does something or don't do something and it depends on certain conditions within them. That can be a certain mentality, a certain capability of intelligence, a certain culture or religion etc. that influences how you behave or don't behave. Techniques that is used, to strengthen the differences, can both be active and action-based (for instance describing a group in a certain way or act in ways to diminish, punish or control the specific group) but it can also be passive techniques with strategies to not see or to not recognize. It can be equally effective to make a group invisible, as to ridicule or threaten the group.

So whilst the ruling groups still consists of an extremely homogenous mass of politicians and decision-makers, which despite knowledge and facts continue to rule our societies with decisions that damages our nature as well as democratic and equal progresses between groups. The governed population is likewise undergoing a continued stigmatization. Differences in gender, age and class has multiplied into differences in most phenomenon in culture, sport, hobbies, careers, education, residential areas, possessions, investments etc. It is all about knowing what is right, in order to gain more influence, but most of us ends up as designated consumers caught up in a rat race where we have been effectively stripped from our democratic power to influence our society as a whole. We are running around in malls to be able to consume whilst we leave the politicians and decision-makers undisturbed to run the world.

Power and principles for Spiritual Social Activism

In a totally equal society the individual will have her full right to shape her own life, given the respect that everybody else has the same right. In an equal society we will first observe the spirit the person is; and then how that woman or man chooses to balance her or his masculine and feminine energies, given such factors as heritage, environment, personality etc., which is that person's own choice. We all have the same need and longing after love, security, respect, joy. Therefore it is natural that we individuals *demands* a positive and constructive societal development, where the politicians of today either adjust according to our demands or leave the power to other people that is more suitable and willing, and will fit into our developments for a positive and constructive life. These demands will not be through threats, violence or aggression, but simply through our democratic rights and through our power as consumers.

Suggestions for mental and emotional actions, in terms of reflecting for yourself and discussing with your tribe following spiritual principles:

o **Power**, concerning our ability to influence other individual's capacity to act.
o **Consciousness**, when it comes to clarify the foundation of every individual's internal landscape.
o **Acknowledgement**, in order to give recognition and express appreciation and gratitude to people in different roles that strives to offer equal rights and opportunities to dialogue for all people.
o **Choice**, in order to clarify all possible opportunities that exist to one individual as well as defending the liberty to select what is desired.

o   **Balance**, when it comes to specially enable someone to receive equitable distribution of time, energy and resources.

o   **Boundaries**, and mark limits of certain behaviour that does not strengthen equality.

o   **Openness**, when it comes to create and maintain unrestricted access to knowledge and information for all people.

Try to clarify the most important spiritual principles and in what way you will honour them.

Suggestions for physical actions for yourself and your tribe:

Change-makers	Evelutionaries
Gather your tribe and create a study group to learn about fair and transparent investments.	Give appreciation to leaders – teachers, sport instructors etc. – who work consciously with equality.
Offer your closest high school to inform both girls and boys about knowledge learnt from your study groups investments.	Offer to be a mentor for a young woman at your work, in a school or in your neighborhood.
Offer young women to be a support when it comes to starting their own business or choose higher education.	Appreciate directly or indirectly positive role models concerning equality, in your city.

6. GROWTH and equal access to dialogue

"I alone cannot change the world. But I can cast a stone across the waters to create many ripples."

Mother Teresa

Growth focuses on all matters in life that is open for individual opinions as well as remains adaptable for development and transformations. It can be hobbies and interests, but it can also be combined with cultural issues like art, literature, music or political debates concerning for instance ecology. In the area of growth we will also find spirituality, religious beliefs, social media and communication in general. Growth is the opportunity for human beings to evolve and transform.

Society has since its own societal birth been involved in a struggle concerning its citizens' free will and civil rights. It is apparently beneficial for a society with intelligent and clear-sighted scientists, politicians and decision-makers, that can enable and sometimes push forward much needed transformation due to new knowledge or conditions. This was for example the case of the findings describing the earth as not being in the centre of the universe, brought forward by Galileo Galilei during early 17th century, although originally based on the work by Nicolaus Copernicus during early 16th century. At the same time it might be the fall of the society itself, with too much new insights and internal critic. Describing the earth as not being the centre of the universe, with the sun and the planets moving around us, was a genuine threat towards the actual perspective of the world and towards the foundations of the church. These brave scientists also had to renounce their beliefs due to

37

this, and it was first in the end of 17th century and in the beginning of the 18th century that René Descartes and Isaac Newton managed to revive and maintain the new perspective on the world, despite the church's reluctance.

The findings of quantum physics worked the same way. Our historical phases are not characterised by sudden and radical changes, but by a kind of rational evolution. We humans have voluntarily changed ourselves according to different techniques of self-regulation. The church was not more willing to change its perspective of the world during the time of Galilei, than during the time of Copernicus. But it wasn't possible to disregard and forbid knowledge during the time of Galilei, which had worked during the time of Copernicus. Knowledge is affected by culture, and is clearly not something universal and historical relative. What we consider to be the truth, is the knowledge that has been accepted as truth. In the same way as radical changes in our society doesn't happen suddenly or unexpectedly, it also hasn't anything to do with influence from geniuses. Instead we may describe it as "contagious diseases", trends of fashion, where small events result in big effects. It only requires certain "rules of ignition" to make it sparkle. One rule of ignition is the "factor of stickiness"; it needs to stick in our mind to stay. Another rule of ignition is the power of connection, where we people basically act like sheep in a herd. We usually act like the majority does, with bad or good results. A certain process of development opens for a new perspective, which creates new behaviours and hence new development, which opens for more new perspectives etc.

There is a constant struggle, or a conflictual process, of societal efforts of repression and opposed forces from groups of individuals or even movements. Societal repression has existed as long as it has existed a need to maintain one kingdoms power, which has transformed from a visual to an invisible punishment and correction. Potential and actual internal and external enemies was visibly punished and tortured, but from 17th century separation and isolation became successful methods to not only suppress individuals unwanted behaviour but to also correct behaviours before it had even happened. This became also a forceful tactic to scare *all* potential criminal and deviant citizens. Social order was created when madhouses, prisons and correctional institutions contained many different (disturbing) groups as beggars, vagabonds, unemployed, whores, mentally sick people and handicapped. A well-structured society was from 18th century born, with anatomical-clinical methods to punish, discipline and correct not only the bodies of the unwanted people, but also the souls. From a relation to God to a subordination to priests to the enslavement from scientific doctors. A disciplinary power was created, extremely manifested in prisons, military camps, factories, schools and hospitals but actually potentially existing in every home.

Thus truth was not only knowledge that experts acknowledged as truth. Experts were slowly redefined to gods with universal rights to make their own decisions and where human beings were subjected to control, punishment and correction. Through constant supervision, with almost immediate punishments or rewards, the goal was "obedient citizens" that willingly adjusted to society, and the means were institutions of governance that had the ability to stop unwanted behaviour before it was even thought of. A transformation has occurred from forces of power and violence to punish and discipline our bodies to forces of knowledge and science to reshape and correct our minds. Most citizens previously accepted a "protective society" for the common good in case of war, famine or plague, but common good for all was slowly changed. It wasn't any more a question of survival for as many human beings as possible, but instead a question of survival for the society itself. Obedient citizens were not disciplined for their own good, so they could both be active and productive workers in good times and be cared for during difficult times. Obedient citizens were the very foundation for the development of society. As loyal bees in a beehive, it is not the joys and developments of the individual bee that is in focus. It is the bee society and the honey that is of interest.

Indigenous beliefs of equal balance of forces and energies

In Norse mythology we can read about the oldest goddesses named *Natt* (Night). *Natt* was black and dark. *Natt* came to marry *Dag* (Day) and together they had a son named *Delling*. Both Dag and Delling was as blond and fair as Natt was black and dark. Like yin and yang the contradictions creates a perfect wholeness and harmony. Natt and Dag also had a daughter, which they named *Jord* (Earth). Our fertile and giving earth is thus conceived by darkness and light. Strong goddesses are in historical documents described as either maternal, wise and reliable or youthful, adventurous and forceful. Mythological stories about these goddesses can be found in many different texts. Historically Snorre Sturlassons *Eddan* (around 1200) as well as the *Poetic Edda* (around 800-1000) is collections of stories that usually is understood as tales of strong men who were fighting each other, but actually is also tales of different strong female figures.

Women were portrayed as strong goddesses, or as equal human beings, where the female characteristics as life-giver, care-giver and handcrafters were important aspects in the society. The roles of the midwives as wise women at births, healing and other care-giving processes were also important roles. Here we can see clear signs of a form of mother-religion, where the women had not yet become "dirty and impure", as they became when Christianity "conquered". Instead the women were seen as key persons in all phases of life. It was the women who carried life and gave birth, and it was the women who took care of the family and of the household through life's all phases (birth, growing up, sickness, pregnancy, and aging).

With the new religion the people started to count kinship on the man's side, which weakened the woman's position. The new god was a man, and he had a son. The Old Testament emphasises again and again that it is the man who is the "true origin" to the children, and the aggression one can find in the texts against women can be interpreted as a consequence of the man's earlier subordinated position. The sex that earlier had been treated as "of less worth" (that is, not the life giver), now turned out to be the single factor of power. Now the important thing was to aggressively conquer the world and fill it with one's seed, which required a young and inexperienced virgin that didn't have another man's seed in her womb. The voluptuous and luxuriant woman with limitless sexual lust, who chose the man she wanted by her side regardless who was the father of her child, quickly disappeared from the picture. Still today this kind of woman is imaged in movie and commercial as a filthy, impure and dangerous woman, only worth despite. Here we can see a clear change of system, a time when the *blade*, as a symbol for the ideology of war, stood up against the *chalice*, as a symbol for the woman. In Christianity the woman was seen as less worth, where the early leaders of the Church even discussed if she could be called a human being. The new religion did not only change the order on the lifecycle of the year, with early ritual celebrations and contacts with the gods, and demanded that all foreign religions should be suppressed, but also the Church should rule over the people and their daily life. It created a clear conflict between the warm and willing goddess *Freja* and the pure and distant Virgin Mary. The woman was seen as full of sin, with temptations, and the hostility towards women was developed that was also increased by the priest's forced-upon celibacy.

The woman's role as a clairvoyant seeress, as a bearer of culture, as a priestess and as a bearer of oral tradition was forbidden, and the independent and clever prehistorical woman was transformed to a weak, unreliable and fragile creature. This even though the messages from Jesus emphasizes a wish for spiritual equality, and with an attitude that is coloured by a humble behaviour, since Jesus told us all to be humble, loving and tolerant. Jesus did not believe that male leaders were the favourites of God, and encouraged his female followers to participate actively in the public life. He also shows himself as the arisen Christ for Mary Magdalene first of all, and asks her to go and tell everybody else what she has seen. In the New Testament there are references about female Christian leaders in the early Christianity. It was also obligatory for a man during the time of Jesus to be married, so if Jesus himself was not married it should have been emphasised in the texts. The most logical conclusion is that Jesus was married with Mary Magdalene. Therefore it is not impossible that Mary Magdalene was one of the leaders in the early Christian movement, which also the *Nag Hammadi* codices suggests, and in some cases openly declare.

In the Nag Hammadi codices there is a different perspective to be found in early age of Christianity on the woman and on equality. Nag Hammadi codices is an example of how the bible really consists of once upon a time chosen texts, since many texts about Jesus was destroyed in the age of early Christianity, if it was not considered to be "the true messages". As it happened a farmer in Nag Hammadi, Egypt, 1945 found a lot of old documents, that in large questions the texts we find in the bible. Even the Dead Sea Scrolls, that during the same period was found in eleven caves in and around the Wadi Qumran in the West Bank, has in fact contents that the Church have tried to cover up to maintain the Western traditional perspective on Jesus and the origin of Christianity. There were during a long time for instance only a very small group of men, with strong connections to the Catholic Church, that were allowed to study the codices.

The Nag Hammadi codices is largely written by Gnostic Christians, that is the Christian people that believed that the knowledge about the mystery concerning the divine truth was something everybody could attain. This group of Christians refused to rank their members in a hierarchy, while the Orthodox Christian early on wanted to separate priests and common members. Wondrous is the courage of Mary Magdalene, who after the death of Jesus dared to challenge the authority of Petri as a self-imposed leader for a new religious hierarchy, where he claimed that only he and his male followers had direct contact with God. Petri was openly critical toward Jesus' perspective on equality already when Jesus was alive, and that was enhanced after Jesus' death, which also explains why the Orthodox Christians considered Petri as the Father of the Church, and neglected Mary Magdalene. The Orthodox Christians was very upset by the Gnostic Christians, which not only considered women be equal men, but also described God as both female and male. For the priests, that saw themselves as "Princes of the Church" - in a kingdom without any princesses or queens - this was too provocative and from the time around 200 AC the "true church" commanded that all copies of Gnostic texts were to be destroyed.

Luckily enough all Gnostic text was not destroyed and we can in Nag Hammadi (now available online) read about God referred as "the blessed One, the Mother-Father, the beneficent and merciful One" or as "the Eternal Light of Knowledge" which seems to refer to the "male side of God" and as "Sophia" – which means wisdom – as "the female side of God". (*Allogenes*, Nag Hammadi codices) Even though it is clearly two different energies of God, it also seems to be with two different purposes.

God is in Nag Hammadi described as "a great androgynous Light", with the masculine name "Savior, Begetter of All things" and the feminine name "Sophia, All-Begettress", also known as "Pistis" (faith). (*Eugnostos, the blessed*, Nag Hammadi codices) Likewise, the human being is also described in an androgynous way, with a soul that has a female nature that is described as a womb. Although the womb of the soul "is around the outside, like the male genitalia which is external". (*The Exegesis on the Soul*, Nag Hammadi codices) The soul however needs to "turn itself inward", to cleanse itself. Surrounding the body, both soul and body will create a whole, as God is a whole with both female and male energies.

It was considered to be a blasphemy for the Orthodox Christians that any common person could reach gnosis, divine knowledge, without the help of a bishop or a pope. It was even more of a blasphemy that the women in the eyes of the Gnostic Christians were seen as independent individuals of their own. Bishop Tertullianus describes during the time of 200 BC the woman as "the devil's door, a false and imperfect animal". The blade came to rule over the chalice once and for all with the destruction or the hiding of documents that enforced the blasphemies. The aggressive attempts of subordination finally resulted in a witch-hunt, from 13th century and forward. The central and wise women in the villages was probably seen as provocative for a church, that at that time had gained considerable power, and therefore the priests dared to try to destroy – eliminate – the clairvoyant women and the shamanic women once and for all. The priests wanted to make sure that the village people could only seek up themselves or the (by the Church educated) doctors for spiritual and physical questions.

In *Malleus Maleficarum* ("Hammer of Witches") written during the years 1486-87 the German monks Heinrich Kramer & Jakob Sprenger wrote about the wise women in a way that resulted in a systematically elimination of women in the numbers from 600,000 to 9 million women, Jews and gypsies (it is of course impossible to know for certain exactly how many it was). The monks meant that women was easier to fall for Satan, since they were fragile and evil, and gave advice on how to discover and punish the witches. It was for instance important to torture the women during a very long time, since they were insensitive for pain and they would therefore endure much torture before confession. There wasn't any reason to consider these women's tears, since witches could not cry but pretended to shed tears with the help of their saliva.

The witch hunt was well-organized campaigns that were financed by the Church; partly to extinct the wise women to help the careers of the doctors educated by the Church and partly to once and for all get rid of the Pagan mother-religions that tried to survive. Today we can with gratitude see that they did not succeed completely, even though they managed to negatively affect our knowledge about the mother-religions and our trust to our own, inner knowledge. Important knowledge about herbs, natural medicine and the creatures in our nature has unfortunately disappeared once for all.

The religion of the old time had a balance between masculine and feminine energy. There was a space for energy and activity, but also for understanding, reflection and community. With time a dominance of masculine energy created ruthlessness and brutality towards those who was not considered to be part of the group. The patriarchal Christianity which in no sense include the true messages of Jesus, is an example of a manipulating and aggressive power. The intuitive flow and the being in now were to be limited, suppressed and smothered. Our dualistic sense was developed, and we lost the sense of companionship and unity with our surroundings. Suspicion, rivalry and competition was created, where the possibilities to live side by side was smaller and the strive to become rulers was more attractive. Our intuition was cut off, and we dared not trust our inner voice anymore. We had lost contact with our own inner leadership. Logic, sensibility and technique was the fundamental stones in our modern society, and concepts like intuition, feeling, reflection and empathy are nowadays seen as something woolly that is connected with "weak women".

Growth and principles for Spiritual Social Activism

Suggestions for mental and emotional actions, in terms of reflecting for yourself and discussing with your tribe following spiritual principles:

- o **Integrity**, so that every individual can align his/her mental, emotional and physical nature.
- o **Vision**, so that a future possibility can be perceived as reality.
- o **Transformation**, to support required actions to be taken to produce the desired result.
- o **Enthusiasm**, to allow strong, inspirational excitement or passionate interest within each and one of us.
- o **Fulfillment**, as in satisfaction for letting individuals working with to the fullest developed ability.
- o **Flexibility**, to be open to take in what might be unfamiliar or willing to change or compromise.

Try to clarify the most important spiritual principles and in what way you will honour them.

Suggestions for physical actions for yourself and your tribe:

Change-makers	**Evelutionaries**
Support indigenous groups to maintain their rights to their belief.	Seek ways to strengthen gnostic wisdom in Christianity.
Make sure there are sufficient knowledge about indigenous groups in schools.	Keep on-going dialogue with and continuous learning from indigenous groups.
Spread new findings in quantum physics in schools.	Seek to understand your possibilities with Quantum powers.

7. BELONGING in Love

*"Human progress is neither automatic nor inevitable . . .
Every step toward the goal of justice requires sacrifice, suffering
and struggle; the tireless exertions and passionate concern of
dedicated individuals.*

*Law and order exist for the purpose of establishing justice and
when they fail in this purpose they become the dangerously
structured dams that block the flow of social progress."*

Martin Luther King

Belonging relates to family, relatives and friends, that is your framily or tribe. Your relationships are the basic for your empowerment.

We human beings are really only relations. We are nothing more than that. We are daughters or sons; sisters or brothers; students and teenagers; employers and employees; husband and wife; mom or dad; grandmother or grandfather. Relations are eternal, like waves that vibrate of connections in eternity. The core in us is based by the relation to ourselves and to God, followed by the relations to our loved ones, that affect for good or worse our relations to our surroundings. Nothing in our existence is without relation, of some kind. I am really "nothing" in this physical world, if I can't see myself from other people's eyes. This is why long time isolation can create a psychical illness, and an unreal feeling of not existing. But of course it can be very different, for each and one of us, how these relations are and make us feel.

We need to move from a culture of obedience to a culture of peace, that is, we need to develop our own inner leadership and stop being obedient towards other, to the point of our own destruction. We need to focus less on ambition, territory thinking, comparing and hierarchies and we need to focus more on intuition, flow, reflection, cooperation, self-esteem, trust and responsibility.

To use your inner leadership is to use your genius. The word genius comes from the Latin word genius, which means "spirit of protection". During 16th century and the Italian Renaissance the spirit of protection was a creature that inspired certain people, and gave them divine inspiration. This originated from Plato, and his perspective on divine thoughts, which created great art and literature. During the Age of Enlightenment the divine aspect was seen as something you was born with, that is, either you had it or not. The concept genius meant something unique and individual. The aspect of genius was seen as irrational which broke against accepted rules. It wasn't talent, since genius was seen more as an intuitive knowledge instead of a rational and structured talent. The genius was considered to have a certain sensibility. The image of genius came to be seen as melancholy or maybe even insanity. It is from this perspective we have the idea that great genius often are unhappy or sick, since the specialness was considered to create an unbalanced development. With the tests of intelligence, which was developed during the 20th century, the aspect of genius came to be translated as high intelligence, which ruled out creativity and intuition as aspects of geniality. The fact is that geniality is depending on flow, creativity and intuition.

We are all affected and shaped by different kind of factors, such as gender, age, religion, ethnicity, class, personality, heritage, genes, social upbringing etc. All of us, regardless of gender, has a certain amount of feminine energy and masculine energy, depending on heritage, environment and social situation. The "perfect balance" to each and one of us is individual, depending on the individual herself. Even if we now are living in a society with patriarchal structure, with a given order of gender where male attributes and qualities is regarded as superior to female attributes and qualities, it doesn't describe men as oppressors. A lot of women, often with careers and/or scientific education, have developed a dominance of masculine energy, which sometimes has caused an oppression of their feminine energy. To develop our true geniality, we need to reinforce our feminine energy together with our creativity and intuition.

We must try to connect the scientific human urge to explain and understand what is surrounding us, with a spiritual insight that we cannot see everything that surrounds us, since there is a world full of invisible miracles. Quantum physics focuses the mystery we have started to realize; we receive more and more astonishing examples on how we humans create the world we live in. This new combination of science and spirituality is essential, when we are trying to change our society. Our society of today now stands at a road junction: either we will perish after hundreds of years of human ravaging against nature and towards animals, or we will manage to unite when we finally succeed in understanding that we all belong together, that we are a holistic unity. The African word Ùbúntù symbolizes this, meaning "I am because you are". I am what I am, since you are what you are. We are united. We belong together.

We have today spirituality without a critic towards society, and feminism without its own, inner spirituality. There is therefore in the society of today an unbalance between masculine and feminine energies. This is due to a process that began when our spiritual belief transformed from gods and goddesses with a natural connection to Mother Earth to the one and only vindictive and punishing god. With this transformation we have also proceeded from self-capable human beings with natural talents to individuals where most power seems to be external in institutions and authorities. For the external power to not be questioned, it becomes crucial to maintain a disbelief in the capability of common people. Our society of today consists of judgemental, punishing and hierarchical rules and regulations, which limits and narrows an individual's possibility to seek within for "the right answers". If we instead create a tolerant, safe and trustworthy society where we encourage our citizen to seek inwards after answers on different ethical dilemmas, we will endorse the development of a spiritually mature individual.

Love is all there is

Photo
By Sophia Lovgren

To belong in love is to belong to life and love life. The love we feel for another person, and maybe for a handful of people, is the same love we need to feel for every person on earth. The intimacy we can feel in closeness and openness with another person, is the same intimacy we can feel for everyone. But first of all, we need to feel it for ourselves.

As world citizens we have a loving responsibility to ourselves, our fellow human beings and Mother Earth with all her abundance to remain and strengthen our independent and critical thoughts and perspectives towards authorities and governments. It is a well proven fact that our Identity as individuals cannot be diminished even though societies prefers us as obedient citizens.

Belonging in pristine mother-religion

During ancient times the existence of the tribe, as well as the elders and the wise, gave us a safe feeling of belonging. During these times it was Fathers as well as Mothers. Also the clairvoyant women (called *sejd* or *völva*, meaning "she who carries a stave" or "she who is clairvoyant") strengthened the position of the women. The clairvoyant women went into trance and told the village people what they should expect, which gave them a central position of power. Clairvoyance was used both for divination and destruction, which could be used for both good and evil purposes. In many cases these women were roving and free people that enjoyed great respect, since their prophecies often proved to be true. These women could affect people, animals and nature, by entering a condition of trance where they could connect with the spirit world. Soul-travelling was seen as something natural for all people when they were dreaming, but clairvoyant women could also with some effort achieve the same magical condition when they were awake. Sometimes it required a "beautiful song", to attract the spirits and to recall the soul into the person's body. This is also something common for shamanic people in Siberia and for the Saami (called the *nåjd*). There has thus been a time when women's natural intuition and creativity was seen as something valuable, as a gift to be used for everybody's wellbeing, just like the men's natural physical strength and concentrated focus.

Clairvoyant women could also change their body, and could either enter another person's body or even more common enter an animal's body. This was something the *aseir Freja* and *Odin* was particularly good at. Changing of body (changing of harbour) has close connection to the Native American's drum travels and use of magical animals. Other similarities is the stave and the drum, important tools to attract the spirits and create magic. People during the times of Vikings also had *fylgjor*, protective spirits in the shape of animals that strongly reminds us of the magical animals of the Native Americans. The Norse Clairvoyants were eventually almost obliterated, mainly due to the believers of the official religion, which were priests who in the Norse Clairvoyants saw a threatening rival for the attention of the people. Also the royal rulers saw in the clairvoyance a form of (with modern words) unparliamentarily movement, with possibilities of political actions and power created by charismatic women and men. Even if it also were men who used Norse clairvoyance, it is clear that this magical practice mainly was used by women. During the same time all over Europe there were myths about the female ability of clairvoyance, and statues has been found of mythical women with staves, that strengthens this theory. Romans used for instance German clairvoyant women, when they wanted help to see the future.

Norse clairvoyance was eventually seen as something unmanly, probably because the phenomenon in itself was close connected to the mother-religions, and included some elements that in a patriarchal, war-loving and aggressive society seemed unmanly, passive and receptive (like trance and healing, that both focuses on a *reflexive accepting* of power and insights from the gods). We rarely hear about Norse clairvoyance today, but still Shamanic people exists. Shamanic people are considered to travel to the other side and communicate with the dead, talk to the animals and heal, and they were common in agricultural societies. The Saami shamanic (*nåjd*) comes from the arctic shamanism, and a *nåjd* can in trance see the future and travel with the soul. Nowadays male shamanic people are more common, which probably has to do with the fact that women by tradition were responsible for the inner sphere. When "strange Western researchers" arrived in modern times, to observe the ancient traditions, it is therefore likely that it was preferably male *nåjd* and not female who these researchers came in touch with. The female *nåjd* exist, in other words, but were not formally observed and written about in historical documents.

Belonging and principles for Spiritual Social Activism

Suggestions for mental and emotional actions, in terms of reflecting for yourself and discussing with your tribe following spiritual principles:

o **Love**, with a universal principle of oneness.
o **Faith**, in devotion for the common good.
o **Unity**, in our state of oneness and gathering for betterment.
o **Intimacy**, with a desire to express love and connection in affectionate relationships.
o **Grace**, in both unrequested protection from harm and unexplainable refinement of movement.
o **Innocence**, since we are free from guilt and fault.

o **Kindness**, where we give without expectation of reward or recognition.

o **Mercy**, in helping people in desperate situation with demonstration of compassion.

o **Service**, to support other people even though it doesn't benefit us.

o **Vulnerability**, when we are open without fear.

Try to clarify the most important spiritual principles and in what way you will honour them.

Suggestions for physical actions for yourself and your tribe:

Change-makers	Evelutionaries
Create neighborhood food teams and eat together.	Put up notes with loving messages around your neighborhood.
Always take with you that you don't need anymore, to give spontaneously to a stranger you meet.	Create a neighborhood library with books that can be borrowed.
Ask a neighbor if they need something at the store, when you are going out.	Create a tribe and send healing love where you gather.

8. PHYSICAL SELF and Energy

"You must be the change you wish to see in the world."

Mahatma Gandhi

Physical Self concerns handicaps, wellness, health, physical safety and disablement, issues of nourishment. We all need to have a positive relation to our body. Our bodies are our instruments here on Mother Earth, which makes us alive and active, and therefore we must dare to *live* in our bodies. Our bodies can be seen as gigantic system of information, concerning many realities, dimensions and time-spaces. Our bodies also origins from material, which is constantly changing energies and foundations with earth, air, water and fire in nature. How can we for instance pay back the water or the air we "borrow" from Mother Earth, which is flowing in our bodies until we die? We even borrow our bodies, which will become earth when we return Home! Mother Earth doesn't demand that we should pay her back, but she requires us to respect the natural cycle of nature and with empathy treat that which we borrow.

The sensuality creates a special bond between the body and the nature. Sensuality in your body is created when you for instance go barefoot in the sand, or touches wood, or you are in the ocean, or you lay on grass or climb on a mountain. Sensuality in your body is also created by physical activities like dance, yoga or hiking, and physical touch like massage. A sensuality that you enjoy is also to be sexual. The womb has a special energy vibration, where life is created and where the forces of universe exist. Foetus in the womb has a special contact with the universe, until they are born. Sexuality, in sensuality, is a divine union of female and male; both between bodies, senses, emotions and dimensions. The sexuality makes us alive and affirmative to life. Sexuality creates life (children, art, pleasure and restitution) in different forms and that which enriches is always right. With the help of our sexuality we can dissolve secrets that are hidden in our cells, like scars and karma from earlier lives and childhood experiences, and by doing this we can unlock our divine consciousness. Sexuality is a connection between heaven and earth.

Levels of oestrogen and testosterone

Does oestrogen and testosterone matter? Yes, even though there is of course also influence from different factors like genetic heritage, the physical biology, the social personality etc. in how we will develop as individuals. Woman was actually in the beginning. All foetuses have only oestrogen when Life is created. For male foetus it is first between the seventh and twelfth week that testosterone is created. When so happens, the boys' brains are being somewhat restructured. Both genders actually have a whole lot of hormones, where oestrogen that is formed in the women's wombs and testosterone that is formed in the men's testicles is two. Oestrogen exists in higher levels for women, and affects amongst other things the ability to give birth and the development of female gender traits. Testosterone exists in higher level for men, and affects amongst other things the sexual urge and the development of male gender traits. There is some uncertainty what testosterone does besides these things, but if you castrate a male animal, he will stop producing testosterone and will not develop any more aggressiveness. The misuse of anabolic steroids (that contains testosterone) also shows that men with a higher dose of testosterone are at high risk to show higher levels of irritation and aggression.

Studies has discovered that the male leader amongst groups of baboons has a unique hormonal influence at crisis. When the group is in danger, the leader's level of testosterone is rising with 50 percentages. But at the same time the level of testosterone for the subordinated males in the group is sinking with 50 percentages. This will thus result in only one aggressive leader, who decides what to do. The same study hasn't been tried on men, it would probably be unethical, but it is a perfect example on group-think. At a crisis the leader rules, with a certain amount of aggressiveness, where the other men will follow with a certain amount of submission. This would be good, if the male leader is reliable and reasonable. Unfortunately many male leaders may be young and inexperienced, when the older leaders has resigned. In a baboon group the old leader's level of testosterone will decrease, and he will join the other subordinated males to follow the new, young leader.

Men and women actually have two different kind of brains. Already as a foetus, when the testosterone is developed, the brain's development will follow one of two models, depending if you are a girl or a boy. The development of the eye will also differ. As adults' men generally have a very good eye sight, but will most of the time only look straight ahead. Women are generally more "broad sighted", and can see better in the periphery. There is also a difference in the inner ear, which enhances the women's possibility to receive and interpret quiet sounds. Studies have also shown that women and men talk different. In a group dominated by men, the members will generally consider themselves to be individuals in a hierarchy. Life is a competition. Men are happy to compete, since this strengthen their sense of companionship. The one who has a high position in the male culture, is the one who tells everybody else what is right. A member of the group will be considered to have a low position if he/she asks for advice, instructions or decisions.

The female culture is characterized by solidarity and involvement. The most important thing is to belong, to be part of something bigger. You will get a leading position if you are liked by many people in the specific group, and you will be forced to a low position if you act as if you are better than the rest of the group. The female language are not as extrovert as the male language. It directs itself to the person the woman is talking to at the moment. The language's purpose is to indicate the speaker's closeness with the one she is talking with. Women also ask all the time. Not because they are uncertain, which men often interpret them to be, but because they want to create solidarity. Of course there are no rules without exceptions, but the fact is that it is possible to see differences. The opposites exist to create a balance for the family; the village; the city; the society; the world. It is important though to be true to oneself and one's own needs, and not to feel forced to behave as others of the same gender, and remain tolerant and emphatic towards other individuals' behaviours and needs.

We can generally see these differences between genders already in early age. Boys plays generally games where you win or lose, and often where you physically compete with each other. Girls plays generally in a certain structure, and not necessary where you need to win. Often you might hear that girls can't play three and three, while it is OK for boys. This can depend on the fact that girls are more unwilling to compete, and prefers solidarity and closeness. When you play three, it is easy to turn to one of the others when you want to say something, and hence you in some form exclude the third person. A girl might feel that she has been excluded, which is central for her participation in the group, while the boy instead will feel compelled to once again get back in the dialogue, in order "to win".

These above differences are possible to trace back to the hormonal dominance you are formed under as a foetus, but it is not only a question about the brain being structured after the hormone which is most dominant. Female foetus who for some reason is exposed to high levels of testosterone (that male foetus are exposed to naturally) will later in life have a more boyish behaviour when they for instance play. Also when you look at the anatomy of the brain, there are clear differences. When you study the brain, you usually do this by studying the flow of the blood in the brain. Then you will notice that men have a greater tendency to only use one of the two cerebral hemispheres. This means that different functions have a tendency to be placed in one of the two cerebral hemispheres. Men generally uses only one hemisphere in a more concentrated matter, which is very important when it for instance comes to spatial tasks and to be able to orientate themselves in the room. Women use both hemispheres equally at the same time, and this is important when it comes to for instance verbal tasks and to be able to hear a word and at the same time see how it should be spelled. The gender difference when it comes to how the nerve cells are storing and transporting different substances, creates for women a better capacity for simultaneous activities, due to a larger amount of connections between the nerves. There are simply more connections in a woman's brain, which for instance means that feelings can be used more often. Men generally have a better ability to find their way around in a large area, where women are better to find their way around in a limited area. Women's centre of languages is in both cerebral hemispheres, while men's centre of languages is in one hemisphere. Men are likely to think with depth, while women prefer to think with width.

Archaeological evidence of worshipping the female body

Even more obvious evidence of mother-religions we will find if we move further backwards in time. Statues of goddesses, or stone amulets like Venus of Willendorf, 20 000 years or so back in time shows us a more plump female body; it is a statue with unshamingly large breasts, a soft belly and big hips and thighs we see. In Scandinavia the evidence is of course of younger date, since the ice made it impossible to create a larger society. Therefore we in Scandinavia have had a patriarchal system a shorter time, which can be an explanation why much of the earlier female-oriented image of the world still exists in modern customs. The Swedish language is one of few languages where we say *she* about the human being. It is clear that what is in focus in these statues and amulets is child-bearing; that which gives life. We don't even know how the ideal man looked like, since we haven't found similar stone amulets of men. These statues show us the woman's important role as life-giver, as do the female-sex-shaped graves show the woman's role as receiver of the death. So what happened? Why did the old cultures transform to patriarchal and Christian societies?

Venus of Willendorf

*Illustration with inspiration
from drawing of statue of
Venus of Willendorf*

By Sophia Lovgren

This change was probably welcomed by the women themselves. In the old mother-religion they were all depending on the goddesses or the whims of nature, which meant that all people had to sacrifice to please the gods. They sacrificed the harvest, the catch, the animals and sometimes the people. It may be that the sacrifices with humans was the reason to exclude the mother-religion, and include the new god that once and for all had sacrificed his own son. There weren't any more human sacrifices required, and this can have been seen as a better alternative with a caring Father that did not demand any more sacrifices but "gave all power to man" (through the priests of course, and as long as the people obeyed the existing rules), instead for a moody and flighty goddess that demanded that the people should be content with whatever they received from nature. Even if the new god, like the old ones, punished the people with for instance bad harvests, the solution wasn't to sacrifice the food you already had a shortage of, but instead to repent through changes in attitudes (the people should simply stop sinning, but they were allowed to continue eating).

We don't only have stories and oral traditions as clear signs of a natural belief in masculine and feminine energies as equal forces. There are also archaeological proofs. Viking graves can be interpreted as such. These ancient "works of art" are in different ways are shaped as female bodies, with the entrance to the female bosom and womb. In the same way one may see the stone ships designed as the female vagina. The thought of graves and ships designed as the female sex doesn't seem unlikely when you consider that birth is closely connected to death, and the fact that we enter life through the womb also should symbolically be visualized as we leave life in the same way. Ships are also symbolically connected to death, since the Viking's funerals took place in a burning ship and since boats often were considered to be the "bridge" from the world of the living to the world of the death. In the same way, of course, we might consider the obelisks', high-rise blocks and canons' (all figures for power, poise and war) symbolic resemblance with an erected penis.

Viking ship and viking grave

*Illustration with inspiration
from photo*

By Sophia Lovgren

Also the Viking graves themselves tells us about the equality between men and women. There are in fact evidence that women also had high positions in the "Viking army", most recently from the Viking town

Birka. The graves contain findings that clearly states the bodies to be of high rank, for instance swords, horses and symbols of strategic and tactic planning. At the same time the bodies themselves shows with DNA analysis, and the structure of the remaining skeleton, that it is women.

We can also analyse the rock carvings from the Bronze Age, that shows dancing women engaged in a rite of fertility. These women's dancing in a circle or on a ship has been found both in Scandinavia and around the Mediterranean Sea. Some rock carvings illustrate the women with bowls between their legs; which is considered to be a symbol of fertility. During this time, and also during the Iron Age, there are clear signs of worshiping the goddesses and of the strong economic and social position of the women. It was natural with such a balance, in a society where it was important with a clan that stuck together and where everyone did their chores.

Physical Self and principles for Spiritual Social Activism

Suggestions for mental and emotional actions, in terms of reflecting for yourself and discussing with your tribe following spiritual principles:

o **Healing**, to return to a state of wholeness by regaining health.
o **Forgiveness**, where we neutralize emotional pain with ultimate acts of love.
o **Authenticity**, with a genuine origin of authorship.
o **Compassion**, where we feel what other feel and offer support or empathy.
o **Focus**, to give sustained mental and emotional energy toward the realization of a desired outcome.
o **Tenderness**, in soft gestures to ourselves.
o **Discipline**, with steadfast adherence to an intention of a desired outcome.

Try to clarify the most important spiritual principles and in what way you will honour them.

Suggestions for physical actions for yourself and your tribe:

Change-makers	**Evelutionaries**
Create a fashion contest "for all sizes" in your neighborhood.	Put up messages about body love in the shops dressing rooms.
Offer free yoga or qigong in the nearest park.	Send healing to food and water in the store.
Gather goddesses for female celebration.	Educate women about natural pregnancies and births.

9. INTELLECTUAL SELF and Personality

"Education is the passport to the future, for tomorrow belongs to those who prepare for it today."

Malcolm X

Intellectual Self has to do with all that which characterizes us; age, gender, sexual identity, physical disablement, ethnicity, individual gifts and talents and intellectual strengths and weaknesses.

Logic, intuition and feelings

Whilst we cannot change our individual levels of hormones, we can affect our different kind of energies. This we can do with the help of logic, intuition and feelings. Our body and our senses speak to us. We make decisions based on at least one of three levels: Logic, intuition and feeling. Logic connects to masculine energy as intuition connects to feminine energy.

- *Logic* can be described as the result of a series of several logical conclusions. Logic is a scientific discipline, with connections to philosophy and mathematic.
- *Intuition* is a tool you can consciously use, when you understand your own feelings and thoughts and when you work with your self-awareness.
- We all have five natural *feelings*; first of all love and fear that can be described as a base, and there after sorrow, envy and

anger which is a consequence of these two. Everything can be divided into love or fear. Love is the sum of all our feelings, and means a total acceptance of ourselves, while fear helps us to be careful and watchful. Sorrow helps us to deal with all kinds of losses, which we will meet in our life. Envy makes us strive towards goal we want to achieve. If we don't allow ourselves to feel envy, that feeling will be transformed into jealousy, envious and grudges. Our anger is a built-in activity of defence, which helps us to say no.

It is important to see that *we are not* our emotions nor our thoughts. With the help of self-esteem and self-confidence we can use our logic and our intuition.

Self-esteem is our knowledge about and experience of which we are, and focus how well we know ourselves and how we relate to what we know. Self-esteem can be described as an inner core, which gives us an ability to rest in ourselves and be content with ourselves. Low self-esteem creates uncertainty, self-criticism and blame. It is as a tendency to "take on the victim jacket" and have a difficulty to choose which people one wants to have in one's surroundings. Self-esteem is an existential quality, a basic tone in our psychological existence, and can be developed both in a qualitative and quantitative manner throughout our life. A good self-esteem makes us competent to handle life's basic challenges and feel that we earn success and wellbeing.

Self-confidence is what we can do, what we are good at and what we can produce. It is more about a taught quality. It is when you have the guts to do those things you want to do, and feel secure in doing them. These both phenomena are of completely different nature, and cannot be compared. If you have a good self-esteem you usually don't have a problem with your self-confidence, but you may have a good self-confidence and a low self-esteem. The problem with a good self-confidence and a low self-esteem, is that you can have a tendency to enlarge your own significance (in relation to the rest of the world), as well as you can reduce your significance. When we enlarge our own significance, we think that people that we know and interact with are sad or angry because of us, and of something we have or haven't done. It may not even hit us that that person can be sad or angry because of something else, which has nothing to do with us. Instead we conclude that it depends on something we said or did, and may not even choose to control if this is correct, but instead act in an angry or impolite way. When we reduce our own significance, we don't understand how well that angry or impolite behaviour is noticed and how much it actually does affect that other person. Our friend may come up to us and ask if it is something, and we act in a rude manner. Warning signals for low self-esteem can for instance be that we do things only to show other people that we can and that we are clever, at the same time as we feel as a fraud, or that we feel that we must compare ourselves with other people even though it means that we think bad thoughts about them, or even say bad things about them.

What we need to do, is to become more aware about our thoughts and emotions, in order to not act upon them nor uncritically "believe" in them. Thoughts are energy forms that support us or destroy our spiritual development. Thoughts contain information that sooner or later will be manifested. We are what we think, since thoughts create and manifest our reality. We can look at thoughts as telepathy, which we send out. It is important *what* we think. Sometimes we think "low thoughts" and these thoughts we can see as created from our personality and from our low self-esteem. Sometimes we think "high thoughts" and these are created by our soul that wishes to develop us. What we need to do, is to avoid the low thoughts, and focus on the high thoughts. This is done to always think thoughts that makes us happy, excited, enthusiastic, proud, loving.

Our emotions are our tools of measurement, which indicate our quality of our thoughts. We need to stay in "the same vibration" as that which we want, to attract it to us. Since we are creators we need to create with intention, according to the law of attraction "equal seeks equal". We will get what we think about, regardless if it is what we want or don't want. Our wishes (to us) must match our convictions (on what we are worth). All we have to do is to ask, and then without restraint let it come. You need to (1) correct your thoughts, so that you focus on all the wonderful things you want in your life, and (2) correct your emotions so that your temperament will fit together with the joy and thankfulness that is natural to have, when you have received all that wonderful things you have asked for. If you focus on what you don't want, that you are worrying about, it is that you will attract to yourself. If your mood goes down, because you deep inside think that you don't deserve what you want, you will "push away" that which you are trying to attract.

We are the source; the unlimited creators and our own masters. We now have the unique ability our inner beliefs so that it is adjusted to the things we want. To be able to do this, it is important that we try to "spend equal time" in different "times of being". As the Healthy Mind Platter describes it, we can for optimal brain matter try to not only focus on the ordinary sections, that occurs in routines: focus time, connecting time, sleeping time, physical time. There must also be time to play time, time in and down time. With other words, there is more than mindfulness besides work, physical training and ordinary responsibilities in our free time for family and household. We must also as adults play and actually also do nothing at all; just be.

Transformation of society and of human beings

How we see the world will eventually change the structure of society. And when the structures of society are changed, individuals' worldviews are changed. How we relate to the world and understand reality shapes our world in many seen and unseen ways. Worldviews are not only abstract, intellectual ideas, but have great implications on our social, economic and political life. Our worldviews inform us about individual choices as well as group identities and it can therefore feel threatening if someone criticize them. It can however be empowering to see other people's worldviews and understand them in a larger context of different perspectives. We can categorize different worldviews in four idea-types, with Annick de Witts model: People with *traditional worldviews* relies in longstanding traditions and conventions, and therefor prefers to trust authorities, often religious leaders or scriptures. Values like solidarity, service to others, humility and self-sacrifice are important, since these people focus on the community and the family instead of the individual. It is more important to take care of each other than pursue your own happiness. Values like honesty, decency, dedication, sobriety and discipline are also important, since obedience to the social roles and rules is of high priority. Often these people see the world as created by God but also as separate from God, in the same way that humanity is fundamentally different from nature and animals. These people are often willing to self-sacrifice and focus on the common good but have great difficulty in accepting change and embracing uncertainty. Connected with this worldview is the Western societal structure of a dominating church as expert institutions, villages as preferred communities and elevated priests as leaders.

People with *modern worldviews* impose views from religious traditions, and prefers to turn to science as the true and reliable source of knowledge. They emphasize rationality, logic and critical thinking and therefore have a very materialistic vision of reality. Reality is what we can observe and life is a product of random, unconscious evolutionary processes. Since most of these people rejects the existence of a higher power or a divine reality, there is a separation between human beings as conscious subjects and the world of unconscious objects. This is the same for the connection between the mind and the body, which leads to tendencies to both prioritize economic, scientific and technological progress and exploitation of nature. These people give high priority to individualistic values, such as autonomy, freedom, success, performance, social recognition and material comfort. Therefore it is important to be independent and self-made. These people will fight for democracy and human rights, as well as the right to pursue your individual creativity and entrepreneurship, but will have difficulty understanding that the choice to rationally prioritize scientific and economic progress is only one choice together with many other choices, for instance the choice to focus on the rights of nature. Connected with this worldview is the Western societal structure of hospitals and universities as expert institutions, excluded parts of a city as preferred communities and doctors and professors as leaders.

People with *postmodern worldviews* understands and respects that there are many different truths and worldviews, since truth is relative, contextual and subjective depending on moral and emotional dimensions. There are multiple perspectives on reality, and this diverse and undefined worldview creates a liberal view on religion and spirituality that can be agnostic or ambiguous. These people oppose the material, technological and scientific emphasis and focus instead on quality of life and values like creativity, uniqueness, authenticity, imagination, feeling and intuition. This focus is often expressed in social movements and rights concerning religion, race, class, gender, sexuality. These people value communities, although not homogenous ones but diverse, heterogenic, pluralistic and multi-cultural communities. Although they respect other views and commit to social justice, they sometimes tend to too much relativism and the opinion that it doesn't exist one truth that has precedence above all other perspectives. Connected with this worldview is the Western societal structure of a social movement or non-governmental organization as expert institutions, local community centers as preferred communities and social movement leaders or successful entrepreneurs as leaders.

People with *integrative worldviews* focus above anything else on the greater whole. This leads to the effect that elements or domains that before has been seen as mutually exclusive, in this worldview are synthesized since it is understood on a deeper level. For example, science and spirituality, rationality and imaginations, economy and ecology, humanity and nature. A larger consciousness or divine reality is uniting all the separate elements of our experience, into spiritual and physical interconnected whole. There is a divine, transcendent force; God is in the world and the world is in God. Nature is seen as having intrinsic value and spiritual significance. There is a great focus on the development or evolution of an individual's full human potential, mostly through spiritual practices, which gives high priority to universal and existential concerns such as life and death, self-actualization, global awareness etc. The holistic perspective of both-and often leads to great social, cultural, economic and technological innovations. These people often overcome dualisms and create effective communication, whilst they commit to universal values and works on self, but they may lack in commitment to engage in political or worldly issues and not be willing to sacrifice for the common good. Connected with this worldview is the Western societal structure of quantum physic as expert institutions, internet forums as preferred communities and the individual themselves as leaders.

All worldviews exist today, within different groups, which is shown in both socio-economic and cultural-historical perspective. One specific country can be identified with several worldviews, often with a previous dominating worldview found in the majority of the population and with an emerging new worldview in the academic or the political elite. This is specifically clear when a political leader stands up, who happens to embody the values of a certain worldview, and a groups overwhelming commitment to that leader. Current examples are Donald Trump and Bernie Sanders, although examples of two opposite worldviews. With a slow change of worldviews, the older perspective might die off a little whilst the newer perspective takes a lead. These processes are continuously occurring in Western society today, and even though it is groups of people who think differently, it is also about worldviews that all have important values and qualities. It shows us how we view life, the world, nature, our fellow human beings and ourselves and thus teach us some profound lessons about our attitudes towards life.

Intellectual Self and principles for Spiritual Social Activism

Suggestions for mental and emotional actions, in terms of reflecting for yourself and discussing with your tribe following spiritual principles:

o **Inner authority**, where we make choices and decisions, with inner guidance, that are beneficial to the totality of the self.

o **Inner strength**, with mental and emotional capacity that support external actions.

o **Willingness**, to be eagerly compliant.

o **Presence**, with focus and concentration what is occurring now.

o **Completion**, in realizing when a process needs to be finished or concluded.

o **Stillness**, and a lack of aggression.

o **Consideration**, in our thoughtful regard for others.

o **Patience**, with our conscious and willing acceptance of misfortune or pain, without complaint or demonstration of loss of temper.

o **Surrender**, and have a state of acceptance.

o **Relax**, as in freedom from bodily or mental work.

Try to clarify the most important spiritual principles and in what way you will honour them.

Suggestions for physical actions for yourself and your tribe:

Change-makers	Evelutionaries
Start up study circles to focus on for instance different worldviews and perspectives.	Make it an agenda to lift up both your and other people's self esteem.
Create neighborhood "newspaper", with news about your local community.	Try to give you and support other people to give equal focus on different time sections.
Create courses and programs that inspires and strengthens use of all time zone.	Gather your tribe for mentoring in both personal and professional life.

10. EMOTIONAL SELF and Neuroquantology

> *"Our scientific power has outrun our spiritual power. We have guided missiles and misguided men.*
> *Life's most persistent and urgent question is, What are You doing for others?"*

Martin Luther King

The Emotional Self concerns matters of self which we combine with new findings and knowledge in neuroscience and quantum physics; neuroquantology.

The understanding of Quantum powers

Our thoughts and our feelings can be defined as energies. The whole universe consists of energies. We can imagine our reality as an energy-field, which moves back and forth in different ways and in different forms. Scientists have taught us that atoms are the building blocks of nature, but maybe we should more accurately describe the atoms as cursory blockage of energy fields. Each atom consists of energy, which you could call "concentrated information". Historically we were taught that each atom consists of vacuum, but that "vacuum" actually consists of more energy than what exists in all materia that exists in the whole known universe. The "vacuum" – the not observable – is in fact the space where it happens most phenomenon, since it consists of an unbelievable amount of energy, that is concentrated information. The materia – the observable – is the place where it happens the least phenomenon. So our focus should in other words be on the not observable. We need to seek our True Self, and encourage a good self-esteem and a positive self-confidence, to develop our spiritual maturity and hence our creative and intuitive flow. We also need to learn to consciously use our power of creation, that is, our energy (in form of visualisation, thoughts and feelings) in a conscious way.

We human beings are only aware of close to 2,000 bits of the 400 billion bits information that we process each second... we are with other words bombarded with information that goes through our senses, and that little amount that comes to our consciousness is that information that serves us first. But the more we open up our intuition and our way to use our brain, the more information we will be able to collect. We are creating our world, and there is no "real" world outside. Our brain is holographic by its nature, and we connect ourselves with the holographic world outside, which means that our perception is processed in the brain *and* "out there". What we perceive in our surrounding is processed in our brain, at the same time as it is processed in our surrounding. What we observe, we affect and with the use of our Quantum powers we will strengthen and understand the process.

The process what we observe we affect means that one and the same particle (that is, processed information) can exist in several places at the same time, which also has been proven by quantum physics. The fact is that quantum physics has been able to show that one particle can be on more than 3,000 places at the same time. Two particles that have been created at the same time are also connected with each other, beyond time and room. What happens with one particle, even if it is thousands of miles away, is instantly also happening to the other particle. This can happen since the particle can be a "solid dot" *at the same time* as it can be a soft flowing wave. We are now talking about particles, that creates atoms, which is the building blocks of nature, which exists in both our body, in nature and in the universe. The decision if the particle shall be a "solid dot" or a "soft wave" is – amazingly enough – decided by the conscious decision of the person observing the particle. In this way we create our external world.

How we think and how we feel haven't only an effect on the now, on our closest surrounding and on our physical and psychical health. Also we *create our future* with how we think and feel. When it comes to this creation of the future, we have all probably heard of the importance to think positive. In quantum physics it has turned out to be impossible to study the smallest particles in a given subject, without interference from the observer, since the smallest particles react on the feelings of the observer. We truly affect and co-create our environment. We can with our energies affect the feelings and thoughts of other human beings, of animals and of nature. We can with our words, thoughts and feelings affect something so small as molecules of water and combined in a large group something so large as the wellbeing of a whole city.

The creation of Quantum genius

Our cells have so called receptors around the external walls, which chemical substances "hang on to". Chemical substances can be naturally created neuropeptides ("molecules of feelings"), that is created by our feelings. We can with other words affect our body with our feelings. This is fantastic in itself, but even more amazing is that our cells quickly can learn to be addictive to those molecules of feelings which are produced most often. We will be addictive to a certain feeling, regardless if it is a positive or a negative feeling. We will also with time develop a tolerance for a certain molecule of feeling, in the same way as with an "external" abuse. We will consequently more often use that molecule of a feeling, in order to "feel good". (In this case it has nothing to do with feelings of love and joy, but with that feeling you want more of.) We must therefore create a specific reality, which creates a specific feeling, in order to satisfy our emotional addiction.

If you change how you look at things, the things you look at will change, might be the best way to describe the above facts. Spiritual change-makers and evolutionaries must unite and together work with matters we want to see in a different way. From environmental problems to war and conflicts; from unfair and dishonest business to oppression and discrimination intersectionally. All is but a thought away from change.

If we don't start to hit the break, and change our perspective, the risk is that Mother Earth is falling apart, and of course we with it. We have already been given alarming signals about a destructive development that is speeding up, both when it comes to animals and nature. And when it comes to us people we are on a good way on ending all our resources. Now it is time to turn inwards, to our own wisdom and magic source of creation, to start building a new world.

Emotional Self and principles for Spiritual Social Activism

Our brain is developed through our senses. Our communication (between our nerve cells) appears to be fantastic. It is not enough that we create our reality with our thoughts and our feelings, when we work with our environment "with the same way of thinking" as we work with our brain. Also our nerve cells can "tell" each other how much of a success the communication was. With other words each nerve connection will in a feedback know how well it has contributed to the process, which makes it the next time create even more nerve connections and produce even more signal substances. It is not enough that we teach the brain which feeling we prefer, by becoming dependant on a certain feeling molecule, but we also teach the brain how well the communication (thoughts, that is memories and experiences) worked with the final result (that is feelings in the body and a resulting action)! This of course works in both directions, that is, the important thing isn't if it is positive thoughts and positive actions, or negative thoughts and negative actions, but if the communication between the thoughts and the actions been effective and filled its purpose. The brain can be said to be "content with itself" if the communication been effective, regardless if you look at yourself in the mirror and thought that you are ugly and disgusting and there after been depressed and sad, or if you looked at yourself and thought how pretty and nice you look and there after felt happy and powerful. Therefore it is of course extremely important that we think positive and there after act in a constructive way.

Suggestions for mental and emotional actions, in terms of reflecting for yourself and discussing with your tribe following spiritual principles:

- o **Divine Guidance**, as in inspiration through contemplation or meditation from a divine source.
- o **Joy**, and to feel and express great delight.
- o **Self-acceptance**, so that you have unconditional regard for yourself.
- o **Self-awareness**, in recognition of the full state of your being.
- o **Self-expression**, and to live authentically from the space of your heart.
- o **Self-respect**, in how you hold yourself within yourself.
- o **Wisdom**, in good judgment.

Try to clarify the most important spiritual principles and in what way you will honour them.

Suggestions for physical actions for yourself and your tribe:

Change-makers	Evelutionaries
Break the barrier between science and spiritualism and become a channel.	Work with Quantum Power in your tribe, when it comes to healing.
Create study groups for inspiration about spiritual economy.	Inspire decisions in your local community to be discussed in circles with talking sticks.
Encourage more groups and political parties to discuss Basic Income.	Develop your non-violent communication.

11. Spiritual social activism

"We think sometimes that poverty is only being hungry, naked and homeless. The poverty of being unwanted, unloved and uncared for is the greatest poverty. We must start in our own homes to remedy this kind of poverty."

Mother Teresa

Spiritual social activism is both an inner and outer process; it is about spirituality and activism. It is not about religion, it is not about any form of dogma. It is activism that comes from the heart, not just the head. It is activism that is compassionate, positive, kind and transformative.

Being a spiritual social activist means taking our responsibility in creating change, with a spirit of positivity, compassion, love and a balance of interdependence and self-determination. Nothing can be more inspiring and more rewarding than being the change we want to see in the world, within and without.

We need to fuse spiritual knowledge with radical action. With our passion for God/universe/Life comes passion for justice and truth, which creates divine love. Lasting joy is devoting your life for others; for the higher good. Act in the world with sacred knowledge and your actions are blessed.

Society of today is now more than ever before effected by stress, discrimination, injustice, environmental challenges, religious conflicts and economic crisis. Neither world organizations nor great leaders seems to be able to create a profound difference in a long-term perspective. More than anything we need our own individual wisdom; we need to dare to be social activists and think freely in order to be able to create and manifest our spiritual solutions. The challenge is that human beings for several thousands of years has been taught not to rely on our own inner wisdom. Instead we have learned to turn to different kind of experts; priests, doctors and scientists. We cannot embrace our Quantum powers, and truly create our new world with our thoughts that become our reality, until we develop and trust our inner leadership. We need to connect our divine spirituality with social and political change. We need to create our external world accordingly to our inner world, that is characterized by truth, joy and love. We need to become spiritual change-makers and evelutionaries, despite fear, disbelief or resistance from our loved ones, our community or society. We need to find our own spiritual tribe and courageously move toward a new tomorrow.

With the holistic model and the spiritual principles for each part, you and your tribe can find tools on how to evolve your spiritual social activism. I have also in this book suggested different physical actions. The holistic model can also be combined with practices and methods of freedom. By using these practices and methods, your tribe will find strength and support in finding its true mission in the world.

Practices of Freedom as general principles of life

The world are full of different techniques to conquer. But what we need is *Practices of freedom*. Practices of freedom reassures us as human beings that we are loved and respected; feelings that are important in our daily life.

Practices of freedom focuses what we want to see as reality in our world, and not what we don't want to see. The practices is created from the fact that we all take responsibility for ourselves, and for our effect on our environment. It requires that we understand ourselves, and our true feelings. The practices of freedom are focused on making ourselves and others seen as the unique individuals we are. Our time on earth will then be an exciting journey in creating our own valuable identity and supporting others in creating theirs. It is also a question about us being respected for the people we are and for how we think. On all societal levels and in all social groups there will with the practices of freedom be a natural openness that welcomes all people. We will constantly strive to respect ourselves and others, for being the fantastic creatures we really are. With inspiration from Ulf Wahlstroms model, we can state that our Practices of Freedom needs to evolve from the following spiritual principles:

☼ ***We are all intuitive creatures, that have a natural right to freedom in shaping our own lives.*** If we are being taught in trusting our own intuition, we may with time understand what is good for us and our environment, which will create a feeling of responsibility and respect for other people's equal right to the same freedom. When we act out of love, from a perspective of wholeness, we can also create a common ethical and moral ground that will cross cultural, traditional, national, international and religious oppositions. We will also learn to be unanimous (in thought, feeling, word and action), where we will affirm our own self and be patient and trustingly cooperate with the flow of life.

☼ ***We will create a new world for ourselves and our environment, through a conscious and voluntary change of attitude.*** The feelings and thoughts we choose, create our reality. Each and one of us are responsible for this process of creation, and for creating joyous constructive and creative goals and decisions that will shape our own and other's lives. By an inner peace and a focus on now we will heal ourselves, which will heal the world and create an outer peace. Decisions that are made are in a long-term perspective, and are created from cooperation and unity.

☼ ***It is in a lovingly and tolerant interaction that we evolve as humans.*** Each human being is teaching us something about ourselves, and even if we don't accept every action we also don't judge the person. Instead we believe that everybody is doing their best from their own possibilities. We treat each other the way we ourselves want to be treated. We learn from our (so called) dark sides, but focus on our inner light. With the help of a language free from values and judgements, we express ourselves kindly, from our own perspective in a straight forward and honest way.

☼ *Our society and our societal economy respects the laws of nature and the natural cycle in nature, which amongst other things create an economy free from selfish interests, inflation and speculation.* We see to the basic need of mankind, which are for instance defined as fresh air, water, food, clothes, a home, warmth and a loving community. A basic income to every citizen, without any conditions, creates a universal right to a security of income, which gives every human her self esteem, her compassion and her natural enthusiasm for a creative and loving life.

☼ *Our society and our societal economy prioritizes respectful human relations, with for example a conscious community planning.* Through a focus on human care in all phases of life, with possibilities of local-based and self-provided communities and tribes, we will recreate a natural way to cooperate and be together which will give an increased life-quality. The society should make it easier for and plan to stimulate human interaction, where we are all encouraged in seeing – and taking care of – each other, from a perspective of wholeness. This will be especially beneficial for children, elderly people and sick citizens, which needs the care and kindness from the larger community.

☼ *A meaningful spare-time is as important, if not more important, as a meaningful employment.* We focus on human's wellbeing and genuin needs instead of short-sighted personal gains and a never-ending increased economical growth. World economy of today can more than ever before for instance allow a general cutdown of a full-time job from eight to six hours. This would first of all be allowed for the majority of people who work in low-income jobs, risking their health and lifes to survive. By doing tgis we will radically change the way we define eachother. We serve each other generously with our work instead of greedy earn a buck from other people's hard work.

☼ *Learning is a lifelong process, where we by encouraging creativity and own initiatives focus self-awareness, loving relations, wholeness and genuin connection in all forms of the learning process.* Human intelligence can be expressed in many different ways, and may with the help of inspiration and guidance be used for the individual's, the society's and the mankind's best. Life knowledge for all ages and all groups, with a focus on a positive self-esteem, a healthy self-confidence and a solid self-awareness inspires to combibe work with joy and peace. Possibilities for lifelong studies and developments of our creativity and inner potential should be seen as equally important as our contributions at work.

☼ *We are all one.* We live in harmony with nature, since we understand that it is one with us. We have a joint responsibility for Mother Earth. Through world cooperation we combine the world's resources after the basic need of mankind. We create environmentally healthy conditions for a long-lasting safe and peaceful existence on our planet, where all people has the right to a certain material wealth and where the love to one another and peace on earth is a reality.

We are all human beings with a soul, a mind and a physical body. With the help of practices of freedom as general principles, we will develop our basic foundation for a spiritual social activism. With concrete methods of freedom we will also find ways how to communicate and express these priciples.

Methods of freedom

Methods of freedom, to maintain these practices of freedom, is for example done by methods for groups to share or make mutual decisions, methods to make long-lasting decisions, methods to choose the right leaders, methods to communicate respectfully, methods to strengthen the voice and creativity of oppressed groups and methods to create a truly economically just and fair society. All methods can be used in a private tribe or a professional business. These are methods that I have summarized down below with the help of inspiration from many different sources.

The Method of Circles is done as a gathering in a circle, for instance to solve problems, share dreams and visions or tell stories, and it is an ancient tradition used by indigenous people. In a Circle you avoid energy demanding argumentation, since the purpose is to communicate with each other in a respectful and loving way. Everyone in the circle has their chance to talk, and if you don't have anything to say you just let the next person speak. In this way, no one has to compete to get the chance to speak or interrupt the person who is speaking. When a person speaks, everybody else give her or him complete attention. When a person is done speaking, the turn goes to the next person. You may use a talking-stick, which is a symbol (for instance a pen, a feather or a ball) that shows "which person has the word". The purpose with the Circle is not to react to what someone else has said, but to show acceptance and tolerance for different opinions. If the Circle has to make a decision, all participants strives to reach a mutual agreement. If the Circle is for sharing, the group continues until no one has anything more to say.

Consider an Native American tribe where they shall make a decision in the "council", that is, the group of elderly people, that patiently discuss the problem. One person at a time is talking, and the talking stick goes to every participant. The decision may be very important, so you let the talking stick go around several times. And then you consider a Western meeting room in a private company where there is a majority of men and a few women. Somebody is definitely the "boss", and there are already some people in the group that knows what kind of decision he wants and that is going to act accordingly. Possibly there is someone else, a brave person, who is trying to talk about other perspective, but angry glazes, sour faces, interruption and a speaking silence eventually wins. The Native American tribe and the Western meeting room in a private company is feminine energy versus masculine energy masked in democratic clothes.

Decisions through seven generations means that every decision must meet the consequences in a perspective for seven generations (a generation is often equal with a man's age). This has for a long time has been self-evident for indigenous people. To create a durable world we need to redlect seven generations backwards, and act seven generations forward. In this way we don't make hasty decisions, but instead our Mother Earth is secured for a long time. According to this traditional perspective, where a generation is equal to a man's age, it is a period of 500 years, that is, the time it takes for a tree to grow tall. In this way mankind is (finally) adjusting itself to the cycle of nature, and don't overload the limited resources of Mother Earth.

Election of "involuntary" leaders is when we choose reliable leaders to create a durable future. Again this is a strategy used by indigenous people. The leaders need to take responsibility for the social, cultural, economical and ecological environment. With a holistic perspective the optimal leadership is by shared leadership, and preferably with one woman and one man. According to the Onondaga tribe it would be too risky to choose a leader that *wishes* to lead, since a leader must take responsibility but also encourage others to do the same. Therefore it is the women, and particularly the Clan Mother, that has the power over the leadership. They raise the future leaders, and the Clan Mother chooses the future Chief (and she is the only one who can dismiss a not suitable leader). She makes her decision on the impression she made after having followed the children during their upbringing. The Council of the tribe gathers, after the Clan Mother's advice, and when there is unity they elect the new leader. He or she is given time to think, since it is an important role that can't be accepted easily. The first task for the new leader is to serve food to all members of the tribe, as a symbolic gesture since he or she shall serve and care for all.

The use of a peace language is when every individual uses a language that origin from her or his own responsibility. What shall be mediated in the language depends on the one who wishes to mediate something, and there should be a profound willingness in being understood and to understand. *NonViolent Communication* (NVC), developed by Marshall Rosenberg, can be described as a language with compassion. NVC is based on the idea that when people feel that their needs are listened to, this will create a common base for contact and cooperation. Through NVC you will learn how to honestly express yourself and emphatically listen to others. You will through NVC free yourself from judgements, interpretations and demands and learn to express your observation, your feeling, your needs and your wishes. With the help of <u>observation</u> you describe what has actually happened, not what you have interpreted (for instance "you came home 9 o'clock yesterday" "hrough our when I waited for you" hat which you observed (for instance "or instance "es. when you free from judgements, interp). With a <u>feeling</u> you describe how you felt towards that which you observed (for instance "I felt alone when I waited for you"). Through your <u>needs</u> you express what you believe that you need, and thereby you take responsibility for your feelings (for instance "I need to know if you are coming late some other night, so that I don't have to sit up and wait for you""). Through your <u>wish</u> you clarify what you wish from the other person and from yourself (for instance "can you please call me the next time you are late?").

Community Work is based on a vision to create unity and solidarity in urban communities; often initiated from the state or the municipal, but in this sense as a need from the people. From an intention to create better lives for the weak groups, you can with Community Work reach out to those who live in the community, and create a physical and/or a social work of change. The purpose is a independent way of thinking, increased self esteem and changed reactions amongst suppressed groups, with message of freedom. People's active participation in mutual matters and freedom in speaking out are stimulated in creative processes, where hierarchical structures are diminished. One concrete example is **Community Reporting**, where you inspire people from socially and economically vulnerable communities to express their feelings and opinions about their communities. Usually social media is popular to use, since youtube, facebook etc. is free or very cheap ways for communication.

Citizen income or guaranteed basic income is an income without any conditions to all citizens, without economical inquiry or demands to actually accomplish any work. It may feel provoking, but this is due to the fact that we in our society have learned that we are all obligated as citizen "to do right" for ourselves. But to maintain that we all must work to survive, is to think that we otherwise would choose not to; that we have a lazy nature. But it is quite evident that this is not at all the case. We are creative creatures and we want to fill our lives with meaning and creation. Just observe any small child when she or he plays; which fills every awaken second with "work". The Citizen income doesn't focus on the family situation (like social welfare) but is a universal right to have an income security, regardless of earlier, present and future incomes. It is not through your performance in the labour market that you earn the right to receive Citizen income, but through the fact that you are a human being with the right to live a dignified life. The welfare state of today consists of a patchwork quilt of unclear, not accurate and not accessible measurements. The Citizen income would simplify the system of contributions, reduce the economical and social costs that are connected to a obligatory close control of the client's self performances and result in a decreased level of arbitrary in the assignment of contributions and support. Everybody has the right to Citizen income, and they who already have a income over a politically defined limit will have the Citizen income decreased according to certain rules of taxes. This will encourage people to work, since you still can earn a decent income besides the Citizen income, but will also mean recognition of so called "unpaid work". Citizen income will secure the citizen's independence, and will also create possibility for their political participation in democratic processes, since we all will be treated as equal participators in a political unity. The Citizen income will prevent exploitation of the weakest individuals in our society, which no longer has to accept unfairly low salary, and thus reduce the trap of poverty and of unemployment. The Citizen income will be paid through societal capital funds and through tax of over-profits in multinational companies. The most important thing is that Citizen income will give human beings back their self esteem, their compassion and their natural but suffocated enthusiasm to create a loving life.

Finally there are many other creative methods to develop your spiritual social activism. With a clear mission of your specific mission in this world, you and your existing or future tribe will find innovative methods that works in your context and for your mission. We need to share generously all creative methods for mutual gain.

12. Spiritual change-makers

"There is just so much hurt, disappointment and oppression one can take... The line between reason and madness grows thinner. Each person must live their life as a model for others."

Rosa Parks

The spiritual change-maker uses yang energy and is therefore focused on societal and individual progress and improvement, often based on principles as justice, solidarity and democracy. This is the typical *Viking Warrior*.

Spiritual change-maker

Illustration with inspiration from medieval drawing of female Sejd (clairvoyant women)

By Sophia Lovgren

The change-makers are always focused on performance and have a high level of activity. Challenges are stimulating. Their mission in life is to enhance consciousness and integrity on earth. They came to support us all in our strive to create a better and more fair world, where we respect each other despite different kind of differences.

A spiritual change-maker is a person who has an idea, that has a clear profit for the common good. In some way this idea will benefit the society in whole, even though it is of course also benefiting the entrepreneur. The change-maker gathers not only resources but also networks of individuals, in order to plan and implement the idea. It is not only a question about the individual itself, who regardless of context and community eventually is successful in getting what she or he wants. It is a person who naturally see the profit in involving other individuals and who immediately see cooperation, context and connections as important as the idea itself.

The change-makers have a high degree of independence and creativity. They don't subject to authorities and have a natural tendency to protest against injustice and rigid systems. They have a strong will and are headstrong, intuitive and psychic. They will easily learn foreign languages, and the question is if this happen in an intuitive way or through the intellect. They can often "see through" other people and they intuitively know when people lie. They are generally sensitive to other people's energies, which can make them appear like insensitive and judging. They yearn to help the world though. They are strongly emphatic, good healers and can easily get in touch with animals. They can have a tendency to quickly get bored and have a hot temperament, since they often feel misunderstood. They are also sensitive to chemicals and non-natural additions in the food.

Depending on the upbringing (since a lot of them easily end up in conflicts) they may be attracted to drugs, and have a tendency to live isolated. If their self-esteem is low they can swing from acting as a victim to feel grandiose. They can also have problems with their sleep, and have depressive periods. The change-makers may have the diagnosis ADHD or similar, since they live fast and intense and are not interested in "slowing down" to meet other people on "lower levels". The change-makers can take care of, evaluate and act upon a great amount of information in a very short time. They like to get to the point quickly, and don't want to waste their time on "social games". Many change-makers have trouble finding a balance in the society, where they can both be themselves and find a place where other people can understand them. One solution is to have their own business, which many of them have since they are very creative. They are the true spiritual warriors.

Develop your spiritual change-maker with Flow & Peak Performance

Spiritual change-makers has a strong ability to experience Flow and Peak performance, due to their intense energy. This will in many ways also help their ideas and goals to come to reality, so a change-maker will do well in often setting up the right conditions to create Flow and ease the possibility for Peak performance.

Flow and Peak performance focuses on self-realisation, which is, when you do something that you like, you usually also is doing something you are good at. And when you do something you are good at, you usually do something you like to do. So, simply put: if you know what you like to do, and that you are also good at or want to be good at, do it as often as you can. The chance is that it will eventually be something you can have an income from, and do even more often. When you do what you like to do and are good at, you have more or less a feeling of Flow, that is, you will feel happy and as if your life is flowing, first described by Mihály Csíkszentmihályi. Even if what you do for the moment being is stuck in some way, it doesn't matter, since you know that you are good at it and will find a solution. The fact is that you may even be inspired by a temporary challenge, and feel that you transcend your earlier ability, when you are trying to solve the problem. Then you can experience peak performance, that is, something miraculous is happening and that which you like and are good at, you are for a short while miraculously "best at".

Flow is therefore a state of mind that can last for a long time, and it can appear every day, if you for instance love to paint and you work as an art teacher at a school. Flow has nothing to do with external success, but focuses your experience of now. The same feeling of flow can arise when you write a book, even if you still haven't been discovered but work as a waitress. But just when you are writing, and you feel the flow, you will intensely let your fingers fly over the keyboard. Small children probably experience flow more or less each day, since they love everything they do, when they play and create, and besides they don't have a reference of what are good or not. Study a child that is concentrated and sits and paint, or happily pour sand into a bucket, and you will know!

Peak performance will arise when you in some magical way feel that you transcend natural laws, and create something that hasn't really anything to do with your intellect or your talent. Like a football player that suddenly catches an "impossible" ball, and in a miraculous way twists his body and keeps it still in the air, and manages to get the ball in the goal in a way nobody can understand. Even if that person is recognised as a good football player, something more happened, than just "being good". You cannot create the conditions for Peak performance to arrive, but you can create the right conditions for Flow.

You can be caught in the feeling of Flow so much so that you are totally open for the divine forces within you, at the same time as you (unconsciously) create your reality, in such a perfect manner that you are not limited to time or space. It is in these times that Peak performance can arise. Keanu Reeve's actions as Neo in *The Matrix*, when he amongst other things are fighting with agent Smith, is a perfect example of physical Peak performance. Of course there are similar Peak performances for all senses and all forms of talents. The common thing for them all is that time stands still, and that the limitations of space no longer seems to exist. Inspiration and creativity flows in such an intense intuitive flow that the forces has blended with you. You are no longer the person that happens to hold such a wonderful tool (your talent), but you are the one that IS that perfect tool.

Flow is a psychic status that arises when a person with enough amount of consciousness and concentration (happily and satisfied) focuses on an activity with a defined goal. You are in Flow when you are creative, concentrated and satisfied with yourself. When you experience Flow you will be totally absorbed in what you are doing, and you will forget time and space. You are totally concentrated, and feel a deep sense of happiness over just existing and doing what you do. Creative and successful people can of course often feel Flow in their creative work, but the fact is that anyone who experiences happiness and satisfaction in a certain situation experiences Flow. Regardless if it is to pick mushrooms in the forest, play with your child or be in an inner dialogue with yourself to be able to solve a problem. To be able to develop your sense of Flow, you first need to notice during which moments you feel well, and then spend time developing this. It is also important to find a balance in the challenge you are about to take, since it can't be too easy or too hard. The result isn't important, but the way getting there is.

Peak performance origins from Flow, and it has little to do with whether you are creative, concentrated and happy for the moment; it has everything to do with whether you feel whole for the moment. In other words, that you use yourself wholly; physically, psychically, emotionally, intellectually and spiritually. The moment you are in Peak performance, you experience it as it lasts forever, and it is an effortless feeling that fills you with magnificent power. You are whole in yourself, in your full power, but you are not aware of yourself. You wouldn't be able to explain what you do exactly, that creates your Peak performance. The fact is that you maybe even wouldn't hear someone ask what is happening, or make the effort to reply, since that which is happening is so totally absorbing you. You are conscious in the now, but not focused on you but on what is happening. Your body is breathing, stretching, getting tense, you lift your hands, you think a thought and you let your fingers perform a will-powered action. You don't have self-control, that is, you don't care if somebody observes you in the moment, and you probably wouldn't even notice that person. You manage to use the *whole* you right there and then, where you with an effortless nonchalance use your creative power. It is obvious for anyone who can see you, that you create your reality. You create magic, and you are in truth magical.

Spiritual change-making and Neuroquantology

Work with the following spiritual principles in terms of reflecting for yourself and discussing with your tribe:

- o **Purpose**, clearly state your intention or determination in your achievements.
- o **Honesty**, and be sincere, frank and free from fraud.
- o **Fearlessness**, in your absence of feeling distress and your strong will in braveness.
- o **Clarity**, and sense of knowing the truth within yourself.

Try to clarify the most important spiritual principles and in what way you will honour them.

You might also work with seven of the nine general intelligences, developed by Howard Gardner:

- Our linguistic intelligence shows itself when we have a great vocabulary, a good ability to talk, read and express ourselves in writings and a talent to learn other languages. It can be obvious when we solve cross words, write letters, is good in explaining connections and appreciate correct sentences. People with a strong linguistic intelligence will without a problem fill in forms and collect fact, and typical professions are politicians, poets, editors and journalists.

- Our logical-mathematical intelligence affects our mathematical knowledge, but also our logical thinking, our ability to plan, to have a schedule, to control budget and appreciate measurements and weights. It shows itself in our feeling for logical patterns and connections, explanations and analysis, and the strive to categorise, classify, plan and try hypothesis. People with a strong logical-mathematical intelligence will be economists, scientists, computer engineers and analysts.

- Our spatial (roomsly) intelligence has to do with a well developed local sense, we will easily find the way and learn maps and diagrams. People with a strong spatial intelligence notices small details in their surroundings, can easily imagine abstract things, appreciates art, fashion and decorations, which is a sense for colour, patterns and forms, and has no problems with parking the car in small spaces. They will happily become architects, interior designers, artists, inventors, hunters and guides.

- Our <u>bodily-kinaesthetic intelligence</u> shows itself when we work with our hands, and use our body in athletic situations and physical challenges, and physically try new things. A person with strong bodily-kinetic intelligence is good at handiwork, hobbies, playing with children, cooking, and remembers more easily that which has been learnt by using the hands than that which has been taught theoretically. It has to do with coordination, balance, strength, flexibility, speed and dexterity and typical professions are dancers, actors, sculptors, mechanics and surgeons.

- Our <u>musical intelligence</u> affects our ability to listen to and express music, to perceive music, to distinguish differences, to change music and to express different kind of music. A person with strong musical intelligence is good at recognising melodies, slogans and verses, and has a feeling for rhythm, melody, sound and tone in a musical piece. Typical professions are something that has to do with music.

- Our <u>interpersonal (social) intelligence</u> has to do with how well we enjoy spending time with other people and how good listeners we are, and how we can comfort other people. A person with strong interpersonal intelligence wants to work with other people, is good at guiding others, mediates in conflicts, and has great patience and a good ability to perceive changes in the mood (that is, sensibility for facial expressions, levels of voices and gestures). These people are happy to engage themselves in organisations and NGO's. (Some call this the intelligence of the heart.)

- Our <u>intelligence of nature</u> affects our ability to understand connections in nature, some kind of ecological ability, and our instinctive understanding for nature. People with this intelligence of nature loves to cultivate and understands animal, they hikes on their spare time, has animals and are good at distinguishing trees, species, flowers.

13. Spiritual evelutionaries

"The best way to find yourself is to lose yourself in the service of others."

Mahatma Gandhi

The spiritual evolutionary uses yin energy and will therefore find strength, creativity and progress by first seeking inwards, to reflect but also to visualize. This is the typical *Natural Healer*.

Spiritual Evelutionary

Illustration with inspiration from medieval drawing of female Sejd (clairvoyant women)

By Sophia Lovgren

The spiritual evelutionaries foremost strength is that of receptivity, warmth, magic and mysticism in all spheres. The dominant traits are nurturing, consideration, empathy, passiveness, non-violence and kindness, where the spiritual change-makers' traits instead would be activeness, boldness and straightforwardness.

The evelutionaries prefers to do things calmly, in mindfulness. Their mission in life is to heal and create balance on earth. They came to help us continue in our effort to create a more loving world. The evelutionaries are characterized by an extensive wisdom that can be shown in their penetrating eyes. The eyes reflect a deep spiritual knowledge. They can very quickly see your inner side, and they think intuitively fast with a natural knowledge about spirituality. There is something pure and innocent with the evelutionaries, since they have an open channel to their highest self. Sometimes an evolutionary can have the diagnose Asperger syndrome, since their vulnerability and sensitivity makes them close their contact with the rest of the world, which they feel they not yet fits in to. They may seem restrictive with feelings of fear, and may feel responsible for other people's pain and they themselves may experience periods of deep depression. A negative "feeling" in for instance clothes, news, pollutions, noises, smells etc. may easily get them out of balance. Therefore they need clothes with a natural material, vegetarian food and not too much electricity around them. Evil deeds from other people may overwhelm them and affect them strongly.

The evelutionaries spread joy and have a warm personality which most people feel comfortable with. They have a magnetic personality and are very affectionate. They can be late with their speech, and may start to sing before they talk, since they are very musical. They can also use telepathy or a made up language to communicate. They have an even temperament and are quickly to forgive. They are very sensitive and emphatic, and have strong healing abilities. They are also very creative, and often have a good balance. They often need to be by themselves, and have a great need of balance and silence, since a large crowd means chaotic energies. They also have a great need of being in the nature and close to water, and may need help to root themselves (with for instance massage). They are often quiet, but can already as children say what they need, and what is good or bad for them. They can also say very intuitive and clear-sighted things about other people. They have a fantastic communication with all kinds of creatures. They radiate and seek unconditional love. It often occurs miracles around them, for instance miraculous healing, and they are fantastic peace agents. They are the natural healers.

Develop your spiritual evelutionary through Image Streaming

The need for reflection, clarifying and energizing might be miraculously heightened if you deliberately use deep meditation or even deep self-healing. By using the different phases in the electromagnetic field, you may thus also strengthen your spiritual evolutionary.

Delta waves moves in the frequency of 1-3 Hz, and are slow, high and broad waves. They exist during deep, dreamless sleep and with awaken infants before they are one years of age. The waves can also exist in trance, for instance deep hypnosis, deep meditation and healing. Delta-waves is a sign that the brain is cutting loose from the physical reality, and seeks "other levels" in quantum reality.

The *Theta phase* (3-8 Hz) is that phase you reach when you are the most intuitive and creative. It is not at all surprising that your creativity is increased when you are at the same level as Mother Earth's electromagnetic field, and the strongest experience you can experience in nature during relaxed meditations. Albert Einstein used for instance "theta fantasising" or Image Streaming, when he during daydreaming let his images flow freely to solve a problem. Then he would receive intuitive answers on how he should move further to get unstuck. For some people it is enough to let the body be relaxed, and let the senses move freely, for the Image Streaming to begin. For other people it can be somewhat more complicated, and they might need some assistance to reach the Theta phase.

Theta waves arises in the border line between sleep and awake, and have connection to the creative process we can experience, with emotionally visualisations. It is here the relaxed meditation exists, and the use of intuition, memory and half awake dreaming. You have here an unconscious entrance to the spiritual sphere, where vivid dreams, insights, geniality and long term learning exist. These waves increase your learning, reduce stress and develop your intuition. You might feel like you are floating away, and as if your senses goes beyond the limits of your body (which it of course does). Frontal Midline Theta is a special frequency at 6.2-6.7 Hz, where people can solve mathematical problems at the same time as they play Tetris, since they see wholeness in a completely new way. At 7.5-7.8 Hz you will reach Schuman resonance, that is your brain waves will be at the same level as the earth's electromagnetic field and you can feel true harmony with Mother Earth.

Also the other waves can benefit your spiritual development:

o *Alpha waves* moves in the frequency 8-13 Hz, and exists in a relaxed adult, that isn't "thinking of anything special". It is here you are calm, creative and visualising in a clear and harmonically flow. You are totally aware, but not affected of fears or worries. You feel free and safe, and you solve problems in new ways. It is a kind of mental clarity, combined with an inner peace. You might even feel a bit electrical and in flow.

o *Beta waves* moves in the frequency 13-30 Hz, and exists when you are awake, concentrated and in cognitive activity. You may be using eye-hand concentration and other visual activities, and your neurones are working hard. You will also remember old and routine-like solutions on problems. Your focus is on studies, training, presentation and analysis. This is the awake individual that analyses its surrounding, asks questions and tries to solve problems.

o *Gamma waves* moves in the frequency 30-80 Hz, and helps the brain to coordinate activities in different areas of the brain. These waves establish a connection of different impressions and create wholeness, and make it possible to create a behaviour the surroundings will accept. These waves are important for learning and memory.

o *Fast brain waves* (80-200 Hz) and *Ultrafast brain waves* (200-600 Hz) is more "abnormal" wave patterns, which for instance exists in epileptic fits but science has yet to explain for us what the true meaning is.

When you want to work with Image Streaming, or intuitive and creative flow of images, make sure you have something that you immediately can describe your images for. A paper and a pen, a tape recorder, or maybe even a friend (that shouldn't talk, but just listen and maybe write down your words). There must be a possibility for you to right away express all the images you see, since the risk otherwise is great that you won't remember what you see, if you wait too long to write it down or say it out loud. You will also stop your flow of images, if you with logic try to cognitively remember. When you start to receive images, feel free to say them out loud, even if you also write them down. Even if it feels like you sometime only make them up, so don't stop. The more you will describe the flow of images, the more clear and alive they will be. Since many images will be symbolic, the meaning of it will be more and more clear, the wider you open your channel. Feel free to talk fast (so that your logical side won't keep up) and keep your eyes shut. A good time length is somewhere between ten and thirty minutes, where you try to describe each image as clearly as you can. That means that you for instance should try to describe each picture from all senses; what you see, hear, feel, smell and taste. You will notice that your creativity will get stronger, the more often you will do this. Besides, this will enhance your intuitive side, since you will "learn" your own language of symbols.

If the above technique is difficult, following advices can help:

- Use an observer: Sometimes it can be the case that you actually don't understand or observes the pictures you receive. Therefore you don't say anything out loud, and since the flow of images is intuitive they will soon disappear. But it is physical possible to observe when a person, who for instance lay still on a sofa, receives images, even if the person doesn't realise it. First the person may hold her breath really quick, when vivid images appear, and second the person's eyes (with the eye lid close) may move faster. (This is "rapid eye movement", not eye lids that is flickering.) What the observer can do at that time, is to ask "What do you see now?". The idea is to help the person observing the images she receives, not to start a dialogue. Thereafter the person herself starts to talk about the flow of images. "Rapid eye movement", REM, appears during the phase of sleep when you usually dream. There is also one form of eye movement therapy against posttraumatic stress, which will activate the system of REM, when the doctor is activating similar eye movements by moving her fingers in front of the patient's face, after that the patient have talked about her painful experiences. These eye movements creates physical changes and activates the parasymphatic nerve system, which will help her work with painful memories.

- Use inspirations: You can also choose to during fifteen minutes look into a wall, or similar, where there is both sunshine and shadows. After that time, you close your eyes, and there will appear patterns and figures in your head, inspired of your observations on the wall. Use these, and describe what you see, and what it makes you think of, and the flow of images will arrive.

- Go behind the first images: It can be that you only see small dots or spots, or that you only hear small noises, and don't think any of those is worth talking about. Still start to talk about them, and see if the report itself doesn't take you further (remember that the logic decision not to tell interrupts the intuitive flow, and if you choose to tell the flow will come back). If you think that you are not getting anywhere, try to go "behind" the spot, and try to "feel" the colour of the spot or "breathe in" the small dots, and see what happens.

- Describe a real image of a memory: Start your flow of images with remembering a real situation, where you in detail describe a wonderful place. It can be your grandmother's garden, your parent's summer house or the island you swam to last summer.

Regardless of what you see, describe it, and when images you don't remember starts to enter your head, you let also these be welcomed and described.

- Use sound: You might be one of those who are most intuitive when there is music that inspires you. Choose your favourite music (instrumental), maybe classical music or relaxing music. There are also nature sounds, which you can listen to when you imaging yourself close a beach or in a jungle.

Spiritual evolution and Neuroquantology

Work with the following spiritual principles in terms of reflecting for yourself and discussing with your tribe:

o **Gratitude**, in showing appreciation for kindness.
o **Tolerance**, concerning your attitudes toward differences of opinion or belief.
o **Peace**, and tranquillity.
o **Gentleness**, as in true humility.
o **Hope**, and optimistic attitude for good things to happen.

Try to clarify the most important spiritual principles and in what way you will honour them.

You might also work with seven of the nine general intelligences:

- Our logical-mathematical intelligence affects our mathematical knowledge, but also our logical thinking, our ability to plan, to have a schedule, to control budget and appreciate measurements and weights. It shows itself in our feeling for logical patterns and connections, explanations and analysis, and the strive to categorise, classify, plan and try hypothesis. People with a strong logical-mathematical intelligence will be economists, scientists, computer engineers and analysts.

- Our <u>spatial (roomsly) intelligence</u> has to do with a well developed local sense, we will easily find the way and learn maps and diagrams. People with a strong spatial intelligence notices small details in their surroundings, can easily imagine abstract things, appreciates art, fashion and decorations, which is a sense for colour, patterns and forms, and has no problems with parking the car in small spaces. They will happily become architects, interior designers, artists, inventors, hunters and guides.

- Our <u>bodily-kinaesthetic intelligence</u> shows itself when we work with our hands, and use our body in athletic situations and physical challenges, and physically try new things. A person with strong bodily-kinetic intelligence is good at handiwork, hobbies, playing with children, cooking, and remembers more easily that which has been learnt by using the hands than that which has been taught theoretically. It has to do with coordination, balance, strength, flexibility, speed and dexterity and typical professions are dancers, actors, sculptors, mechanics and surgeons.

- Our <u>musical intelligence</u> affects our ability to listen to and express music, to perceive music, to distinguish differences, to change music and to express different kind of music. A person with strong musical intelligence is good at recognising melodies, slogans and verses, and has a feeling for rhythm, melody, sound and tone in a musical piece. Typical professions are something that has to do with music.

- Our <u>intrapersonal (reflexive) intelligence</u> has to do with a great well being in being alone and enjoying one's own company. A person with a strong intrapersonal intelligence has a good ability to plan her time, understands her own reactions and feelings, is enjoying independent work, and knows directly what is good or bad for her, reaches goals, loves to day dream and fantasies and reflects a lot on how useful her experiences will be. These people has a good self discipline and are aware of their weak and strong sides. (Some call this the intelligence of the soul.)

- Our intelligence of nature affects our ability to understand connections in nature, some kind of ecological ability, and our instinctive understanding for nature. People with this intelligence of nature loves to cultivate and understands animal, they hikes on their spare time, has animals and are good at distinguishing trees, species, flowers.

- Our intelligence of existence has to do with an interest for the great questions in life. A person with this intelligence of existence reflects a lot over life and death and is happy to discuss religion and philosophy. Typical professions are of course priests and likewise, but they might as well be atheists or agnostics.

14. You, Creator of Worlds

"It is better to lead from behind and to put others in front, especially when you celebrate victory when nice things occur. You take the front line when there is danger."

Nelson Mandela

We cannot only work with ourselves, and thereafter be content with that. We also need to take a conscious position for our loved ones, for our fellow human beings, for nature and for Mother Earth. A spirituality without societal criticism is nothing else than cosy navel-gazing. A societal critic without spirituality is nothing else than a mission without ethical purpose or wholeness. We need to create our tribes, to inspire each other to live conscious lives with social activism. We need our tribe to be a strong force, as political citizens and economical consumers. It is important that we remind each other to visualize a better world. Choose to focus on what you want to exist, not on what you want to erase. Where attention goes, energy flows. Be constructive in your own actions; your power is enormous.

In creating our tribe it might be both strengthening and inspiring to agree upon some basic perspectives. Basic spiritual principles will help us establishing the platform, on which we stand when we gear our way through life.

☼ **We know that there is an original force that has created us, that we can connect to when ever we want, which gives us an inner sense of security.** What we call this original force is not interesting, but the important thing is the unconditional love we receive and can choose to give. We also know that we in this life on earth may be affected by different kind of problems, but it is not something we "deserve". Instead it is based on choices we have made, which has created certain consequences, which we can learn from to increase our insights. Regardless from our life situation we are taken care for and loved by this original force, which is strengthen and enhanced by a positive and loving visualisation.

☼ **We know that we are all created by this force, which makes us all brothers and sisters.** This insight creates a self-obvious love and emphatic behaviour towards other people, instead of looking for possible shallow differences. We want to support each other in showing our next best version of our higher self (where the absolutely best version is in spirit world, the real world, where imagined phenomenon like war, starvation, robbery, murder, competition, greed, stress etc. isn't real).

☼ **We are all godlike, and our soul is for ever.** We are joy, truth and love. We learn constantly and we develop all the time. We learn from other people, for better and for worse, which makes judgements, condemnations and critique pointless actions. We are all made up of the same loving force, and from our feeling, which is the language of the soul, we will once again become aware of what we have always known, but for a moment forgotten. We are creators, and may in this life know by experiences what we by concepts always have known. We experience our godlikeness and for love to be able to be experienced, we must have a (constructed) opposite. We are here to remember, and genuinely experience what we once couldn't experience but only knew.

Intuition and synchronicity as Quantum powers in tribe process

Intution and synchronicity is vital parr of your Quantum powers. We have even started to receive scientific proofs of our Quantum powers. Quantum physics has shown that consciousness resides in a field surrounding the brain. This field is in another dimension and transmits wave information. This wave information, now called Quantum Wave Resonance, encompasses all neurons as well as the mental field and transmits all information instantly. With other words we have a mind field that exists around and outside our physical brain, which communicates with our brain. So the ability to "pick up" other people's feelings and intentions with our own huntches, which we may define as intuition, is now an explainable process describable as Quantum powers.

I have been talking about Flow and Peak performance, which at large part origins from your creative actions. But also when you are not creating, you can experience flow, and this you will do with the help of your intuition. This you can sense in conversation with someone; in a decision you are about to take or before something important you are about to do. Your intuition is the flow in your life, and demands some self-knowledge. You need for instance to understand your own fears, to know when it is your intuition that speaks to you and when it is your fears. The intuition exists only in the now, and origins from your power to control yourself. Your fears origins from the past. You will know what is what, if you give yourself time to sit down and listen to yourself. You are in truth your perfect inner leader. Through intuition you will express your true self, and create your true self, in a perfect and effortless flow. With the help of your intuition you will instantly notice *how it is*, without using your experience or analyse with your intellect. Intuition requires with other words feminine energy, which can be one reason why we say that women has more ability to intuition. Of course it is not true in one sense, men has as strong intuition as women, *if* they open up for their feminine energy.

Intuition works instantly. It flows to you without any effort, and if you are trying to receive the intuitive messages stronger or force yourself to feel more intuitive messages, the most part will be lost. Intuition only exists in the being of now, when you react on situations with ultimate (effortless) efficiency, and when you are in touch with your inner voice. If you try to force it, you exist in the doing, and that is not where the intuition is. "Ultimate efficiency" doesn't mean that you gain time, money, resources or similar. There are no such conscious thoughts, when you are intuitive. Instead efficiency focuses an effortless, flowing and self evident perspective to that which is coming to you and to that which tells you how to act. Actually everything is very simple; either it feels good and true, or either it doesn't feel good or true. So if you decide to only do that which feels good and true, you will have success in all areas in your life. But unfortunately as we know it doesn't work that easy, and it has to do with our constructed fears. We think with our intellect what we should do, depending on what the surrounding has taught us, instead for only listening to the higher intelligence, which through our inner guiding system tells us it *is* good when it *feels* good. When we do this, we manifest events and things in a flow that doesn't seem to require any effort at all from our side. We interact from another level in our being.

A particular aspect of our intuition is **synchronicity**, first introduced by Carl Jung, that is "casual" coincidences in our physical surrounding. It can for instance be events that are not at all depending on each other, or inflict with each other, but still reminds of each other. You can for instance on three different occasions, while you go to work, meet different ladies that are all wearing pink coats and have a black dog in a leash. The event in itself should be noticed by you, and lead to a reflection on what that was all about. It can also be words, names, people, animals, vehicles, countries etc. During one day you might in the morning meet a man from Nigeria, and then at lunch you receive a book which focuses Nigeria, and in the evening when you look at TV you will see a documentary about Nigeria. What it might be will show itself to you on several occasions, in a "random" way, but which will in some way or another have some significance for you. The more we are in a intuitive balance, the more often this synchronicity will occur. It is an instant connection between your thoughts and feelings and what is happening in the world, which has to do with the fact that we are all energies that exists in an energy field. We simply interact with our God-consciousness, and at that moment we are very powerful creators. Through synchronicity we will receive messages, which will help us in our life, regardless if it is from higher guides or from your higher consciousness.

There were a research project conducted at Princeton University, called Global Consciousness Project, where the existence of a collective conscious field was studied. This project had an certain amount of "eggs" (Random Number Generators, RNG), around the world, which generated electronical noise through random sequences from a large amount of the numbers one and zero each second. These sequences created a constant curve, which appeared the same in all eggs, and which repeated itself according to the same pattern almost the whole time. But sometimes an international event would occur, which made a large number of people to consciously focus that event, and then the curves would change and produce a greater turn. With other words, collective thoughts and feelings changed the electronical noise which these eggs picked up. We can all influence our surrounding energy field, and if we think and feel the same thing, we will become extremely powerful in our creation.

For us to use our intuition more often, we need to "loose our senses". We simply need to move from our intellect to our "gut feeling", that tells us to act in a certain way. Intuitively strong people will say their intuition comes from the area around the stomach or around the heart (our centre with solar plexus chakra and heart chakra), while others talk about a buzzing feeling around our forehead or back head (third eye chakra). You can't use the logic in your intuitive flow, because then your intuition will stop, so it is better to "accept it all" and then after the moment has passed try to judge what you have received. If you after you have decided to follow your feeling, feel stillness within, you can be certain that you have followed your intuition. If you, after your decision to follow the intuition, feel no need to double check with a friend, you can calmly continue in the intuitive flow. Each time you decide to follow your intuition, you will strengthen it. That is because you "confirm" the intuition and you learn to recognise the process and therefore gets more secure in your intuition. And each time you follow your intuition, try to observe exactly how it feels, when the intuitive feeling came. What physical sensations did you experience? Where in your body did you feel it the most? Try to remember them, so you the next time can feel even more secure. The more you get to know yourself, with faults and forces, the better you will be in following the intuitive flow. Use your tribe to together strengthen your intuition both individually and in your group. By doing this, your tribe will become an intensely strong group.

True power and your life purpose

We human beings are here for the sake of love. Rest in your soul, in the eternal moment of now, and stop for a second to think, feel and do. Be content with just breathing. What we need is first and foremost love. The amazing force that is created in this magical behaviour, makes all fears disappear and tears down all barriers, and reshapes us to the genius goddess-creators we are. We are small eternal lights, fantastically beautiful in our glory, always shining in joy, truth and love. We choose to come down to this place, for the feeling of experiencing and creating. Our soul creates and "understands" that which the brain cannot grasp. We "only" need to follow our feelings and live our truth, to become the Masters we actually already are. By understanding our natural energies, that is not influenced by gender, age, race, class or ethnicity, nor physical health, sexual identity, wealth, education, status, occupation, we might find our basic foundation for understanding our life purpose and our mission in life. What we now need is a new paradigm and a culture of peace, where we live in a natural cycle with nature, and where we are encouraged to true self-expressions, a qualitative equality and an inner leadership.

Let's continue the dialogue, cause the journey has just started!

www.sophialovgren.com
www.spiritualsocialactivism.com
www.visionarylife.se

"A strange passion is moving in my head.
My heart has become a bird
which searches in the sky.
Every part of me goes in different directions.
Is it really so
that the one I love is everywhere?"
Rumi, Looking for Love

The one I love is everywhere

Photo
By Sophia Lovgren

The Thunder, perfect mind

Nag Hammadi codices

I was sent forth from the power,
>and I have come to those who reflect upon me,
>and I have been found among those who seek after me.
Look upon me, you who reflect upon me,
>and you hearers, hear me. /.../
For I am the first and the last.
I am the honoured one and the scorned one.
I am the whore and the holy one.
I am the wife and the virgin.
I am <the mother> and the daughter. /.../
I am the utterance of my name. /.../
For I am knowledge and ignorance.
I am shame and boldness.
I am shameless; I am ashamed.
I am strength and I am fear.
I am war and peace. /.../
I am the one who is disgraced and the great one.
Give heed to my poverty and my wealth. /.../
But I, I am compassionate and I am cruel.
Be on your guard!
Do not hate my obedience
>and do not love my self-control. /.../
I am the one who has been hated everywhere
>and who has been loved everywhere.

111

I am the one whom they call Life,
      and you have called Death. /.../
I am the one whom you have hidden from,
      and you appear to me.
But whenever you hide yourselves,
      I myself will appear.
For whenever you appear,
      I myself will hide from you. /.../
I am the knowledge of my inquiry,
      and the finding of those who seek after me,
      and the command of those who ask of me,
      and the power of the powers in my knowledge
      of the angels, who have been sent at my word,
      and of gods in their seasons by my counsel,
      and of spirits of every man who exists with me,
      and of women who dwell within me.
I am the one who is honoured, and who is praised,
      and who is despised scornfully.
I am peace,
      and war has come because of me.
And I am an alien and a citizen.
I am the substance and the one who has no substance.
Those who are without association with me are ignorant of me,
      and those who are in my substance are the ones who know me.
Those who are close to me have been ignorant of me,
      and those who are far away from me are the ones who have known me.
On the day when I am close to you, you are far away from me,
      and on the day when I am far away from you, I am close to you. /.../
I am control and the uncontrollable.
I am lust in (outward) appearance,
      and interior self-control exists within me.
I am the hearing which is attainable to everyone
      and the speech which cannot be grasped.
I am a mute who does not speak,
      and great is my multitude of words.
Hear me in gentleness, and learn of me in roughness.

I am she who cries out,
>   and I am cast forth upon the face of the earth.
I prepare the bread and my mind within.
I am the knowledge of my name.
I am the one who cries out,
>   and I listen. /.../
I am the name of the sound
>   and the sound of the name. /.../
For I am the one who alone exists,
>   and I have no one who will judge me.
For many are the pleasant forms which exist in numerous sins,
>   and incontinencies,
>   and disgraceful passions,
>   and fleeting pleasures,
>   which (men) embrace until they become sober
>   and go up to their resting place.
And they will find me there,
>   and they will live,
and they will not die again.